NOT SUCH A BAD GUY

BAD BOYS OF THE BAYOU

ERIN NICHOLAS

ISBN: 978-1-952280-45-0
Cover Design: Najla Qamber, Qamber Designs

AUTHOR'S NOTE

I've been published for over a decade and have written a lot of books in that time. I actually don't know how many. I've counted a few times before but there are short stories and novellas, bonus material, things that have gone out of print, or been re-worked… and I don't know how to count all of that. I usually say, "over fifty books" and figure that's safe.

But in all of that vagueness there are a few things that have become what I call my "orphans" over the years. Books and stories that don't really *belong* anywhere specific anymore. I was first published with Samhain Publishing which has since closed its doors, and all of those books came back to me, including stand-alone stories that didn't connect with anything else. I've also had some really amazing opportunities to participate in various projects and events and series for which I've written a story (or stories) and I've enjoyed them all! But projects end, and opportunities shift. So, over the years, projects, series, and publishers have come and gone. But the stories are still alive and well. They just don't really *fit* anywhere.

So I finally decided that I needed to give them a home. And a new chance to meet readers! They needed a new place to live. But I needed to put them all together and give them a connection to one another since they didn't have other connections.

And, where else would I make this new home than Louisiana?

Now I couldn't just bring these people (some of whom I've known since before I was published!) to Autre, the home of my other Louisiana books. They don't quite fit there. They have a different vibe. They came from a little different Erin Nicholas. Not totally different, of course. My voice and style have always been pretty consistent.

But these stories are a little grittier. More emotional. The people have a little more baggage than the Boys (and girls) of the Bayou or the people of Boys of the Bayou Gone Wild. They're also a little dirtier. There's always open-door sex scenes in my books, but in Bad, Louisiana, there are just more of them. These books just have a little different feel. And they needed their own home. Their own place to live and be what they are rather than trying to fit into something else.

So, I present to you Bad, Louisiana. A collection of books that have existed in Erin Nicholas world for a long time but have been rewritten and edited to fit together in a new town, with some new friends, for a second chance to meet readers and bring even more love stories to the Louisiana bayou!

I hope you enjoy them as much as I did when I first wrote them and loved them again going back for this reimagining.

If you're a long-time reader and are "afraid" that you might have read these books before, you can check out the original titles and more information here: https://bit.ly/BadBoys-ThenNow

WELCOME TO BAD, LOUISIANA!

These boys are only called "bad" because of their hometown...

Yeah, right.

I've been to Bad several times over the years and it always makes me smile. The town itself has an interesting history. It was originally, and very briefly, settled by a bunch of Germans. Did you know that Germans use "bad" in town names to denote a spa town? Yep, that's a thing.

So, I guess in this case, there was a small hot spring outside of town and the settlers claimed that made it a spa town in the new frontier. They named the town Bad Salzuflen and they'd hoped it would attract even more settlers. Particularly of the young and female persuasion.

But, unfortunately, the 'hot spring' was actually just a particularly marshy area (no one knows why it was so much warmer... or at least they're not saying) and then, before they could figure out what to do about that, the French showed up and ran the Germans out.

Well, after that no one could pronounce or spell Bad Salzuflen, but they didn't really want to go to the trouble of renaming the whole thing, so they just dropped the Salzuflen, painted over that part of the welcome sign, and the town decided to lean into the whole *Bad* thing. Especially in more modern times.

Seriously. The hair salon is called *Bad Hair Day?* (yes with a question mark so that when they answer the phone it's, "Bad hair day?" and you say, "Yes", and they say, "Come on down and let us fix it!" And there's so much more.

Here's a quick list:
Bad Habit—coffeeshop
Bad Brakes—auto mechanic shop
Bad Brews—bar and restaurant
The Bad Egg—diner/ cafe
Bad Gas—gas station and convenience store
Bad Faith Community Church—local church
Bad Hair Day?—hair salon
The Bad Place—the physical therapy clinic
Bad Medicine—the medical clinic
Bad Memories—community center

Instead of fighting it and letting everyone else mock them, the citizens decided to have some fun with it. And hey, they sell a lot of merch (like *I got Bad Gas on my roadtrip* travel mugs and *I've been to The Bad Place and survived* t-shirts) and no one ever forgets a trip to Bad!

So come on in and have some fun! It really will be a *good* time!

THE SERIES

You can read the Bad Boys of the Bayou in any order!

The Best Bad Boy: (Jase and Priscilla)
A bad boy-good girl, small town romance

Bad Medicine: (Brooke and Nick)
A hot boss, medical, small town romance

Bad Influence: (Marc and Sabrina)
An enemies to lovers, road trip / stuck together, small town romance

Bad Taste in Men: (Luke and Bailey)
A friends to lovers, gettin'-her-groove back, small town romance

Not Such a Bad Guy: (Regan and Christopher)
A one-night-stand, mistaken identity, small town romance

Return of the Bad Boy: (Jackson and Annabelle)
A bad boy-good girl, fake relationship, small town romance

Bad Behavior: (Carter and Lacey)
A bad boy-good girl, second chance small town romance

Got It Bad: (Nolan and Randi)
A nerd-tomboy, opposites attract, small town romance

NOT SUCH A BAD GUY

A fling, a funeral, and a little falling in love... just another weekend in Bad, Louisiana

Physical therapist, Christopher Gilmore is back in Bad, Louisiana, for the reading of the will of his friend and mentor, Patrick Faucheaux. Christopher expects a small memento from the man he considered a father figure. He gets far more—including the task of sorting through Patrick's belongings with the help of his beautiful, sassy daughter, and fellow PT, Regan.

Who just happens to be the woman with whom Christopher had a hot, spontaneous encounter in a bar storeroom the night before.

Awkward.

And amazing.

Like all the residents of Bad, Regan grew up adoring Patrick, which made learning he was her father—just days before his death—feel like the ultimate betrayal. She wants nothing from the man who cheated her out of having a father, and even less from his adoring ex-student. Too bad she can't get Christopher's kisses out of her head.

Forced to work in close quarters, Regan and Christopher succumb to their scorching chemistry as they sift through Patrick's life, learning things about him neither knew—both good and bad. As Regan's bitterness toward her father fades, Christopher's admiration for the man also dims. Discovering his role model was a flawed human after all has Christopher questioning his judgment in other areas…like his feelings for the man's daughter.

Is his attraction to Regan the real deal? Or is this all just a really bad idea?

CHAPTER ONE

"OH, honey, I love you *so* much!"

Christopher Gilmore wasn't expecting the gorgeous girl who had been sitting at the end of the bar for the better part of the last hour to declare her love for him so early in their relationship. He also hadn't been expecting her to *actually* throw herself at him. But he was a very intelligent guy, and when he found his arms suddenly full of soft, sweet-smelling woman—whether he knew her name or not— he thought fast.

And kissed her.

Which she seemed totally fine with, if the way she kissed him back was anything to go by.

She might have intended it to be only a hug, but amazing opportunities were meant to be grabbed. Not that he was grabbing her. Exactly. But his hands did fit very nicely over the curve of her ass.

And she definitely wasn't protesting. He felt her little sigh, he felt her run her hands into his hair, and he definitely felt her open her mouth under his and meet the stroke of his tongue with hers.

She smelled like buttercream frosting. He'd swear it. And he wanted to lick her from head to toe. And those two things were, actually, not related. He would have wanted to lick her from head to toe no matter what she smelled like. The kiss was that good.

Damn, he loved this town.

Despite its name, nothing bad had ever happened to him in Bad, Louisiana. Not one thing. Because of that, and because he'd found his passion for his life's work here, Bad held a special place in his heart.

Gorgeous women who smelled good and felt even better? Now Bad was for sure his favorite place in the world.

Christopher was still sitting on his barstool, but she'd stepped between his knees as if she'd been there before. She'd wrapped her arms around his neck and pressed her body to his as if she really was madly in love with him. And she was now kissing him as if maybe she'd forgotten she had never done more than smile at him across a bar.

She seemed to remember a moment later.

She pulled back abruptly and stared up at him. "Holy crap," she breathed.

Christopher grinned. A reaction like that could fuel a guy's ego for a while for sure.

"Regan?" A big guy with more tattoos than hair moved in behind her, a scowl on his face.

She looked into Christopher's eyes, licked her lips and whispered, "I'll owe you."

Regan.

Blue eyes.

Soft brown hair to her shoulder blades.

Buttercream frosting.

Denim-covered ass that fit perfectly in his hands.

Yeah, he could handle her owing him.

He gave her a wink.

With a little inhale and a smile, she turned. "Oh, hey Kurt."

She was still standing between Christopher's knees and he

decided that whatever he was playing along with required his hands to stay on her hips.

She seemed to agree. She leaned back slightly, settling that sweet ass against his groin.

He coughed and shifted slightly. Damn. She was cute and kissed like a wet dream and he was two beers in and in a great mood, but he was still surprised by how quickly all the blood in his body rerouted to the area behind his zipper.

"Hey." Kurt's eyes went to Christopher.

Regan pressed back more firmly and Christopher's body answered with a counter pressure that was less intentional.

He shifted again on the bar stool while also moving her slightly to the right. She put her hand on his thigh, resisting moving even an inch and making their pose look even more intimate.

"I didn't know you were back in town," she said to the other guy.

Christopher didn't even know her and he could hear the tension in her voice.

"Just rolled in," Kurt replied. "I came looking for you first thing."

Now Christopher *felt* the tension in her body.

"Why is that?"

She flipped her hair back, no doubt in an attempt to look casual, and the air around Christopher stirred with the scent of sugary frosting.

Kurt's eyes narrowed. "Because I'd hoped you'd be waiting for me."

Regan's fingers tightened on Christopher's thigh. "I don't know why you'd think that. We went on one date and it was a year ago."

Ah, an ex. Kind of. A spurned lover. Or a spurned lover-wannabe. Christopher got it now.

"The only reason we didn't have a second was because I got arrested."

A spurned-lover-wannabe *felon*. Great. What had he gotten into here?

"That wasn't the only reason," Regan told him coolly. "But yeah, that didn't help."

"It was just a misunderstanding. You know that."

"You stole my car, Kurt."

Christopher felt his eyes widen. Okay this was…interesting. It wasn't assault or arson or a bank robbery. Could be worse. Still, he was a little less pleased now about her choosing him as her pretend-whatever to avoid Kurt the Con.

Kurt shook his head. "I *borrowed* your car. Without asking first. That's why it was only a misdemeanor and why I'm out already."

Regan took a deep breath. "Are you seriously trying to tell me—"

Christopher pinched her hip. No reason to piss off the guy off. Who knew what he'd learned in prison?

"Cupcake," he said calmly. "How about I buy Kurt a drink and we all forgive and forget? He's out and starting a new life and you have me."

Regan stiffened, no doubt in surprise—though whether it was over the pinch, his term of endearment, or the suggestion in general, he wasn't sure.

But she turned and smiled up at him. "That's a great idea. I'm going to go to the bathroom. Be right back."

And she slipped out of his arms.

Oh, no. She wasn't leaving him here with her ex, the criminal. Who was clearly not happy that Christopher was with Regan. Hell, for all Christopher knew, *she* was a criminal too and this was a set-up to get something out of him.

He snagged her wrist, hoping like hell she wasn't a criminal. "Maybe I'll buy Kurt a drink and then meet you back there."

He said it suggestively. Very suggestively. So suggestively that everyone who heard it knew exactly what he meant. He might as well have said *How about a quickie in the ladies' room while Kurt nurses his free beer and contemplates his poor life choices?*

"You two are together?" Kurt asked, before Regan could say anything.

"We are," Christopher said, not taking his eyes off of her face. "Seems like since I first set eyes on her, she's all I can think about, and from the moment I first kissed her, I can't keep my hands to myself."

Her eyes widened slightly and he saw the hint of a smile curl one corner of her mouth.

Well, it was all true.

He'd noticed her right away. He'd already eaten his burger and was making his way through a half pint of his favorite beer—one that he couldn't find back home and only one of the things he'd missed like crazy since he'd last been in Bad—when she'd taken the seat at the other end of the bar.

She was beautiful and had a sweet smile and, well, that ass in those jeans, so he'd made note of her immediately. But then she'd ordered the same beer, and over the course of the next hour had put Chase Rice on the jukebox—four times—and had laughed at the same jokes from the bartender that Christopher had. All of that combined for Christopher into "a little smitten".

The bartender, Marc Sterling, who also owned the bar, had been chatting with them both over the course of the hour in between serving others who came up to the bar. It was a weeknight, but Bad Brew's was the only bar in town, so it was still busy enough that Marc was jumping from one order to another. But he'd get a few minutes breather every so often and he would chat with Christopher or Regan, the only two permanently seated at the bar rather than the wooden four-top tables throughout the room.

Christopher remembered Bad Brews fondly from his previous time in Bad. It was named, as were most of the businesses in town, with a tongue-in-cheek use of the word "bad". There was The Bad Egg, the diner where he'd had many an amazing breakfast. He'd needed his car worked on at Bad Brakes. He'd gotten his hair cut at Bad Hair Day? And, of course, he'd done his internship at the physical therapy clinic, The Bad Place. That one was, of course, his favorite. He'd met very few PT patients who would not agree with that name for a therapy clinic. He'd bought three of the clinic's t-shirts because of the name alone.

But he'd also spent some time in Bad Brews when he'd been here for his three-month rotation and tonight, more than ever, he appreciated the way everyone seemed like old friends even if they'd just met.

Over the past hour, listening in on Marc's conversation with Regan, Christopher had learned she liked fried pickles, loved chili cheese fries, had lost money on her fantasy football team, and had hated the recent Ben Affleck movie.

Christopher assumed she was from here. She and Marc knew a lot of people in common, anyway. He supposed she could have moved to town in the two years since he'd been here. He'd only been here for three months two years ago but there was no way in a town this size he wouldn't have run into her. And he definitely would have remembered her.

He should have made a trip back before now, obviously.

For just a moment, Christopher's heart squeezed as he recalled why he was here. He'd never been to a reading of a will before. He should have come back before now for more than the beautiful new woman in town.

"I'll take a Sam Adams," Kurt said, climbing onto the barstool next to Christopher and jerking his attention back to the current situation.

Kurt was going to take Christopher up on the offer of a beer. Okay. But they weren't going to bond over that beer—or over their shared infatuation with Regan.

Christopher lifted a hand to Marc. "Sam Adams," he said, pointing to Kurt. "On my tab." Then he swiveled his stool toward Regan, who he still held by the wrist. "Let's go."

He wasn't really going to accompany her to the bathroom. But he was going to use her as an excuse to escape Kurt's company. He wasn't one to judge. He saw all kinds of people in all kinds of situations as a PT. Many of those situations were unflattering and people were not at their best. But he knew he and Kurt had exactly two things in common—they each had a Y chromosome and they both had a thing for Regan.

No need for them to further their association beyond those things.

Heading to the restrooms might have been Regan's idea, but Christopher took charge as he stretched to his feet and started toward the back of the bar. He kept his hand on her until they were safely around the corner from where Kurt was sitting and tucked into an alcove where they could be as alone as possible inside the bar.

But as he swung around to face her, he was hit by those big blue eyes and those soft lips and, dammit, that sugary-sweet smell that made him want to eat her up.

"Thanks," she said before he could speak.

His first instinct was to say *my pleasure* and it wasn't out of simple politeness. He certainly hadn't minded being the one she'd chosen to lock lips with.

"You tried to ditch me back there with him," Christopher said. "Not cool. After everything I've done for you."

That hint of a smile teased her lips again. "Everything you've done? You mean not outing me to Kurt as a girl you just met?"

"That," he said with a nod. "And the kiss."

"You did that *for* me?" she asked.

He shrugged. "I'm assuming you're a lonely spinster. Maybe even a virgin. Who hasn't been kissed in a long time."

Her eyebrows shot up, but he could tell she was still fighting a smile. "Quite an assumption."

"Educated guess."

"Do tell…what makes you so sure I'm one, lonely, two, a

spinster—and do you even know what a spinster really is?—three, a virgin, and four, not up on my current kissing?"

He liked her.

It hit him suddenly. He was attracted to her, loved kissing her, loved *smelling* her, and now he liked her too.

Even if she did date criminals.

He gave her a slow grin. "Well, you don't have a boyfriend, or he'd be in here with you and you wouldn't be kissing strangers to avoid exes, and that kiss…well, that was the kiss of someone starving for it."

He was teasing her. He didn't even know her. How did he feel comfortable teasing her?

Her eyebrows rose even higher on her forehead. "Starving for it? I wasn't the only one in that kiss, buddy. That kiss was very two-sided. And, if you hadn't glued your hands to my ass, I might not have…" She trailed off and her cheeks got pink.

He chuckled. "Might not have what?"

She seemed to be considering her words for a moment. Then she said, "Kissed you like I was starving for it."

He laughed louder that time and drew the attention of the few people standing closest. He took her by the shoulders and turned her so her back was against the door marked "storage" and he could cage her in. And block out the rest of the room. He suddenly wanted a few private minutes.

Or hours.

"Sorry about my hands on your ass." He wasn't. At all.

He could tell she knew that.

She smiled a full smile this time. "I forgive you. Completely."

"So…no boyfriend? I was right about that part?"

"You were," she conceded with a single nod.

He was very happy to hear that. He loved being right. "How about the spinster part?"

"You think I'm past the age where I should be married?"

"Is that what a spinster is?"

She pursed her lips, wrinkled her nose and nodded in the

cutest expression he'd ever seen. And cute was not a word Christopher Gilmore used on a regular basis outside of puppies and penguins. Even newborn babies, contrary to popular opinion, were not cute. But he really liked penguins.

"So that's a no then," he said. "That leaves only one assumption not cleared up."

"Ah yes, what was that again?" she asked.

God please don't let her be a virgin. Because suddenly he wanted to see what else she was starving for. And he didn't really want to be the first.

"The virgin thing," he said.

"Right. The virgin thing," she repeated. Her eyes were twinkling.

Had he *ever* actually seen twinkling eyes before? "Right."

"Not a virgin."

He let out a breath he hadn't realized he was holding.

She ran her palm over his left pec, her attention focused on her hand. There was a layer of cotton between her skin and his but he felt the heat and friction all the way to the soles of his feet. She looked up at him and Christopher wanted to run the pad of his finger over the tips of her lashes. That was a hell of a thing to want.

"And I would really like you to kiss me again."

Heat and want grabbed him down low. "You have a thing for bad boys though. And I'm a really good guy."

He was. It wasn't just that he'd been told that over and over…and over. And over. All his life he'd been a good guy. But he liked it. He liked being the nice guy, the trustworthy guy, the heroic guy.

"Bad boys?" She frowned. Then her forehead smoothed and she gave a light laugh. "You mean Kurt?"

"Your ex-con ex," Christopher said with a nod.

"One date," she said firmly. "It was a dating-site thing. It was awful even before he stole my car."

For some really stupid reason, Christopher hated the idea

that she was on a dating site. Not that he had anything against dating sites. But because he hated the idea that there were a bunch of guys out there looking at her photo, learning things about her, asking her out.

He didn't want anyone taking her out.

And what the fuck was *that*?

"So you just attract creeps," he said lightly.

She laughed softly. "As a matter of fact…"

He snorted.

"But you don't *seem* creepy," she said.

"And I'm definitely attracted."

"It was the Chase Rice, wasn't it?"

He chuckled. "Yes. But the fact that you laughed at a joke that started out 'a nun, a rabbi and the Pope walked into a bar' sealed the deal."

They stood grinning stupidly at each other.

Finally Christopher said, "But this still might not be a great idea." It really probably wasn't. He was in town only until Sunday. He was here for the reading of a *will* for God's sake. A one-night stand hadn't been part of the plan. "I mean, *you* could be the creepy one," he said lightly. "I don't know that I won't end up tied up in your trunk or something."

Though putting this woman and rope together in the same thought didn't go down the ransom-note pathway but veered immediately toward the satin-sheet-and-slow-jazz pathway.

She seemed to be pondering his comment. She gave a serious nod and said, "Then I guess we're just going to have to stay here so you feel safe."

Before he could figure out what she meant exactly, she reached behind her, turned the knob on the door she was leaning against, and pulled him into the storage closet.

CHAPTER TWO

SHE WAS REALLY GOING to have sex with a stranger in the storage closet at Bad Brews? *Really?*

But the moment the door shut behind him, the man's mouth was on hers and there was no way she was leaving that room until that mouth had been on a lot of other places.

She'd known she needed something tonight. The past few weeks had *sucked* and she'd felt like everything had been building up in her like a pressure cooker. Something had to give. She was a regular at the Bad Brews. She liked their burgers and she and her friends came by all the time for margaritas. But she hardly ever came in by herself and bellied up to the bar.

Tonight she'd needed…something. Beer had been her first thought. Or something stronger. Loud music. Conversation that had nothing to do with her father. Maybe even some dancing.

It looked like the Bad Brews had exactly what she'd needed after all.

And this high was definitely stronger than the beer could offer.

The guy kissing her in the dark storeroom seemed to be on board. His big hands slipped under the bottom edge of her t-shirt and he ran his palms up and down over her waist before pulling her up against him more firmly.

She gladly went. Being up against him was exactly where she wanted to be right now. He was gorgeous. He was tall and lean, but solid, with hard muscles under his basic cotton t-shirt and well-worn denim jeans that she wanted to rub her…everything…against. He had a great smile, an even better laugh, and great taste in beer. He also had deep green eyes that held intelligence and humor. Light brown hair. An easy smile. And big hands that, maybe stupidly, seemed confident and strong. Could hands seem confident and strong? Could she know that from simply watching him lift a beer glass and feeling them squeezing her ass for two minutes? She wasn't sure, but those were the words that came to mind. Good words. Words that made her hot.

Confident and strong were two things she hadn't been feeling for a while. Even before finding out the secret of whom her father was…

Regan instantly shut those thoughts down and tuned back in as the guy's hands blazed a hot path up her back and around to cup her breasts.

She pressed into his touch and he ripped his mouth from her. His breathing was heavy, or maybe it was hers, as he ran his thumbs over her hard nipples. "My name's Christopher."

She laughed lightly even as electricity seemed to trip along her nerve endings from her nipples to…her entire body. "Hi, Christopher. I'm Regan."

"I'm here—"

"No!"

He froze, hands still on her breasts but not moving.

"Sorry," she said quickly. She covered the backs of his hands with hers. "Sorry. I just…no details, okay? Let's just mess around. We don't need to be friends. Or see each other again."

A terrible thought occurred to her, followed by *would that really be terrible*? "Are you new here?"

"No. Yes. No," he said. He sighed. "I've been here before. I'm just visiting this time."

She let out a relieved breath. Okay, she wasn't going to run into him at the grocery store. That was a plus.

So why did a little voice in the back of her head say *dammit*?

"Great. Then this can be just a little fun for tonight," she said.

"Yeah," he agreed. "Right. Just a little fun."

She pressed his hands against her breasts and then ran her hands up his arms to his wide shoulders. "I'm having fun."

The light that spilled in under the door was not nearly enough to help her actually see anything in the room, but it kept it from being pitch black. She'd never been *in* the storeroom of course, but she'd gotten a quick impression when she'd pulled him inside. It was about ten by ten, two walls were lined with shelves, a third had brooms and mops and a few folding chairs propped against it and the fourth was empty except for the door. That was the one she wanted Christopher to put her up against while he did dirty things to her. Things that would distract her from the thoughts that felt as if they'd been spinning for the past thirty-two days.

"I'm having fun too," Christopher told her, sounding amused by the fact.

"You let me know if you *stop* having a good time," she said. She reached between them and pulled her t-shirt over her head.

"I'm not expecting that to happen." His voice was a little gruffer now.

He couldn't see her, but he obviously knew she'd stripped her shirt off. Especially when she tugged his up over his stomach to his chest. He lifted his arms and let her pull it the rest of the way off. She let it drop, anxious to get her hands on his skin.

He was hot and hard. Those were the first two words to occur to her as she ran her hands over his chest and down his rib cage on either side to his flat abs. Hot and hard were also good words.

Regan reached behind her and unhooked her bra, letting it fall to her feet. Then she stepped forward and pressed her breasts to his diaphragm, relishing his hot and hard parts against her hot and soft parts.

She took a deep breath, rubbing her nipples against his chest.

"Jesus," he muttered. His hands splayed over the middle of her back and held her close, as he slowly dragged his chest back and forth against hers.

The light, crisp hair over the hard muscles sent shocks of need to her core and she gave a little moan.

He pressed her closer and took her mouth again in a kiss that had her wrapping a leg around his and trying desperately to get closer. Though there wasn't much getting closer. As long as they had clothes on at least.

He moved a hand between them, taking her bare breast in his palm and kneading before taking the nipple between two fingers and tugging gently. At the little whimper she gave, he tugged harder and Regan felt as if she was melting.

"Damn, Regan."

She loved the gruff mutterings. In the dark room, it all felt deliciously naughty, and she loved being able to only hear and feel what was going on. She was affecting him. She loved that. He didn't feel sorry for her; he didn't have any opinions about her personal life or judgments about her family and parentage. He wanted to spend time with her based on simple things like her taste in beer, music and her sense of humor. And okay, maybe her willingness to get naked with him in the storage room.

Still, that was all a lot easier to handle than the questions and speculation she'd been getting from the people she knew. His words, the funny and the hot ones, were way more appealing than the words of "comfort" she'd been getting since her father's death.

Christopher's hands were now back on her ass and he was lifting her.

Regan easily focused her attention on the man who was pressing her against the door, just as she'd wanted. She wrapped her legs around his waist and welcomed the pressure of his impressive erection against the seam between her legs.

She kissed him with a hunger she hadn't felt in a very long time. She wondered if he could feel the gratitude in it. Because there was a lot of that too. He was taking her away from the awkward, confusing, anger-and-regret-filled past month.

He stroked his tongue into her mouth, just aggressive enough that she squirmed against his cock, needing so much more.

He dragged his mouth down her neck, hiking her higher against the door as if she weighed nothing. She grasped his upper arms, the bulging of his biceps making her even wetter.

"Christopher," she said breathlessly.

She didn't know what she meant to add after that. Probably *fuck me,* which might be a little much. And might be a little soon. She wouldn't mind all of this going on for a while.

Then her nipple was in his mouth.

Her head thunked back against the door behind her. Oh yeah, this could go on for a while.

His tongue teased her first, which was enough to have her throbbing with need. Then he closed his lips around the hard bud and sucked.

She had another hard bud that could use that same attention.

"Christopher."

Was that her voice? That pleading whisper? Yeah, had to be. But she didn't remember ever sounding like that before.

Then he scraped his teeth lightly over her nipple.

The next noise was obviously from her as well, but she was *sure* she'd never made it before.

"God, I love how you sound." He sucked on her nipple again then kissed his way to the opposite side. "How you feel." He licked. "How you taste." He sucked. "How you smell." He did the teeth thing again.

She gripped the back of his head. "Don't stop."

"No worries there, Cupcake."

Her head came off the door. That name again. It had sounded

pretty sarcastic to her earlier in front of Kurt, but this time it sounded like a true endearment.

"Cupcake?"

"You fucking smell like a cupcake. And now I know you taste like one too."

She laughed lightly, somehow. "The lotion doesn't taste like cupcakes."

"It's a lotion?"

"New. It's called Buttercream Frosting."

He paused for a moment and then laughed, the hot hair puffing against her breast and making her nipple tingle as much as his tongue had. Well, almost as much.

"What?" she asked.

"Buttercream. I knew it. It was my first thought."

She grinned at that. "Really?"

"I love buttercream frosting."

She wiggled against him. "But it doesn't taste like it. Does it?" She hadn't actually *tasted* the lotion.

"*You* taste like it. With or without lotion. You're sweet and soft and delicious." He proved it, by dragging his tongue over her nipple again.

She squirmed. "That's so good."

"So good," he agreed.

She could picture his smile.

"But you know what this means," he said, pulling back.

Pulling back was *not* okay. She clutched at his shoulders. "No."

"Yep." He let go of her legs and her feet swung to the floor.

"*No,*" she protested, arching against him. "Christopher."

"Sorry. I gotta know how sweet you are all over." His hands went to the front of her jeans.

Her brain was only half a step behind. He had her pants unbuttoned and unzipped before she moved to help him push the denim to the floor.

His hands cupped her ass and Regan wanted nothing more than for him to rip her panties off and make her come.

The thought was sudden and kind of shocking. She wasn't typically a do-me-hard kind of girl. She actually wasn't a I-need-it-bad kind of girl either. Sex was okay. She had orgasms some of the time. Even when she didn't, she liked it okay. But it was rare that she felt as if she *needed* it.

She did now.

She reached for his fly as well, praying that he had a condom close. She was definitely not a carry-a-condom-around kind of girl.

"Do you—"

But before she could ask, or do more than get his zipper down, he went to his knees.

And she forgot about everything. Condoms, the fact that she'd barely had a chance to really check out the width and length he had going on, or the question about how any of this was really going to work—because she also wasn't a sex-against-the-wall kind of girl.

He pulled her panties to one side and put his mouth on her.

And Christopher whoever-he-was became her favorite person in Bad. Maybe the world.

Regan slumped back against the door as waves of pleasure rolled over her. He seemed happy to lick her as if he was licking buttercream frosting from a spoon, and Regan felt her legs widen of their own accord and her hand somehow tangle in his hair without any conscious command from her brain.

Because her brain wasn't doing anything but saying *oh my God I want this forever*.

The licking was...delicious. And not a first. But it definitely felt like a first.

And then he sucked. Right on that hard nub that had suddenly become the center of her existence.

That was all it took to make him her favorite person in the *universe*.

Because about five seconds of that, combined with the little flick of his tongue, and she was up and over that beautiful edge and diving into an orgasm unlike any she'd had in recent memory.

A low moan that sounded like his name filled the room and she realized it was her again.

She also realized that she was pulling his hair. Hard. And that he seemed not in any hurry to leave where he was.

She tugged his head back and sank to her knees in front of him. "Holy crap."

"Second in one night. Nice." He sounded amused. And smug.

She didn't mind. He deserved to feel smug.

"Let's go for a third." Regan went for the front of his pants as if he was hiding chocolate chip cookies in there.

What he had was even better. She got her hand up against the hot length of him and they both moaned.

With a muttered curse, Christopher got to his feet, pulling her up with him. In the process, she managed to shove his jeans and underwear to his knees.

"Hang on, hang on." He was breathing raggedly as he fumbled for his jeans. "Condom."

"Yes!" Her reaction was possibly overeager, but she immediately went for the pocket on the opposite side of where he was rummaging. She came up empty. "You do have one, right?" she asked. Did she sound panicked?

Maybe just horny.

He chuckled. "I appreciate the enthusiasm. Need my wallet."

"Wallet?" She frowned and went digging, but he'd already snagged it. "Isn't front pocket more convenient?"

"Yeah, well, I wasn't counting on you tonight, Cupcake."

She paused at that and admitted he had a point. And that was probably good. She'd rather not be in here with him if any girl who came along would have been in this same position with him.

The stab of jealousy at that thought made no sense.

Things that made no sense seemed to be her norm lately though.

"But you do have one?" she asked.

He chuckled again and she heard the soft *whump* of leather hitting the floor. The wallet. Then she heard the crinkle of foil. *Yes!* But she kept that one to herself as she slipped her panties off. Lest he think she was sex-starved or something.

Though she *felt* sex-starved. And maybe she was. Did six months without make someone sex-starved?

She felt him shifting and then his hands on her butt again. He lifted her against the door and she assumed the condom stuff was taken care of.

"I can't believe I'm doing this," he said softly.

"Me too," she admitted. It was true. And she was sure later she'd be all kinds of embarrassed.

But that was later.

"But I really want you to do it," she said, putting her lips to his neck. "And do it hard, okay?"

A shudder went through him that she sincerely hoped was lust.

The next second she was pretty sure that was exactly what it was, because he thrust, hard, filling her up. The groan that accompanied it was heartfelt and that sound alone made her inner muscles tighten around him.

But that groan, with the friction and the heat and the simple dirtiness of having sex in the Bad Brews storeroom, all combined with the memory of his grin and his eyes and the way he'd laughed and teased and gone along with her crazy pretend-to-be-my-boyfriend thing to make her entire body shiver and tighten.

He didn't move at first and Regan felt her body clenching as if trying to pull him closer.

"Damn, this won't last long I'm afraid," he said roughly against her ear. "You feel too damned good and you sound like every fantasy I've ever had and I can still taste you on my tongue."

Her body clenched at that too.

"And then there's that," he said with a half-groan, half-chuckle.

"If you don't want *that*," she said, flexing her inner muscles and getting another groan. "You gotta stop talking dirty."

"I don't think I can." He flexed his hips then and she felt the tiny thrust through her whole body. "You make me want to say all kinds of dirty things."

She wanted to hear every one of them. "Well, it's not like we can stay in here all night. Hard and fast is best. So let's hear what you've got."

His hands tightened on her butt and he said, "How about I don't think I've ever wanted to fuck someone as much as I want to fuck you?"

According to her pelvic muscles, that was pretty good. Her brain agreed. As did every cell in between the two. "Yes. That," she said, sounding far too breathless already. "More of that."

He held her tight as he pulled out and then thrust forward again. Wow. She didn't remember sex feeling so good. And he'd only thrust twice so far.

"You're so tight, so hot, so wet," he said huskily against her ear. He thrust again.

"It's never like this," she heard herself say.

"And see, *that* kind of talk works really well for me," he said, moving in and out again.

"You like hearing you're amazing and the best I've ever had?" she asked, trying to keep her tone light.

It was sex in a storage room. In a bar. With a guy whose last name she didn't know. How could this be the best?

Of course, his timing was impeccable. Not much going on in her life had been what she'd label as the best.

"I like hearing anything in that sweet, breathless voice you've got while I'm buried deep," he said.

Okay. Well, in *that* case.

"Harder, faster, more," she said.

He squeezed her ass. "You know what you're getting into here?"

"Let's find out."

He did exactly what she'd asked, she'd give him that. Holding her firmly against the door, Christopher pulled out and sank back in, deep and hard. He repeated the motion several times in a row, nice and fast. Regan felt the orgasm gathering deep and she tightened her thighs around his hips.

"More," she panted. "More. Please."

He gave a muttered "fuck" and pulled out.

"Hey!" she protested. "I—"

He let her slide to the floor. "Turn around." He didn't wait for her to move on her own. He pivoted her to face the door. "Hands up." Again, in spite of his command, he moved her hands to the door, pressing her palms flat against the surface. He kissed her shoulder, his hand sliding up her arm, down over her breast, where he tweaked her nipple, then down over her stomach to her clit. "Take a deep breath, Cupcake," he said gruffly as he circled her clit, then slid two thick fingers into her hot channel. "You're about to get a lot more."

Then his hand was gone and he was gripping her hips, tipping her ass up slightly and then thrusting deep into her, hitting a spot that made her want to weep.

He held her tight and fucked her. Exactly as she'd asked. Exactly the way she needed.

She was already climbing to the peak three strokes in and by the time he returned his finger to her clit and pressed, she was on the edge. His finger and the low "what I wouldn't give to spread you out with the lights on" sent her flying again.

He continued to stroke in and out, deep, hard and fast, and a minute later he gave a growl as he came.

They stood, still joined, breathing hard for several seconds. The heat and fading ripples of pleasure made Regan wish she could just sink into a mattress, turn over and go to sleep. She was spent.

And it had been a few stolen minutes in a closet.

If there had been a mattress, more room, more light—she might not have been able to walk out after.

She chuckled softly.

Christopher shifted behind her and pulled out. "Laughter? Really?"

But she could tell from his tone that he wasn't actually offended.

She heard the rustle of clothes and as she turned, she felt soft cotton against her breasts as he handed her t-shirt over. Her nipples tingled just having his hand that close.

"I was just thinking about this thing I saw on Facebook," she said, crouching to feel for her bra and underwear. "Something about if he thinks you can get up after sex to make him a sandwich then he did something wrong because you shouldn't even be able to walk."

"I'd agree with that," Christopher said.

She grinned. "So no sandwiches with you. Good to know."

"But you're especially tough, you might be able to handle it. I just made you come so hard I had to hold you up while I finished and you're thinking about some damned thing on Facebook."

She gave a surprised laugh as her fingers found the strap of her bra. Being in here this long had helped her eyes adjust and she could see his dark form stepping into his underwear and jeans.

"I don't know if I came *that* hard," she said as she stood.

He was in front of her a split second later, backing her up against the door. "Then I'd better try again."

Damn, she wanted that. Now. Here. Again.

She wet her lips and shook her head. "I don't think that's how bar quickies go."

"You're an expert in bar quickies?"

She laughed at that. "Um, no. I'm just guessing. The word 'quickie' kind of implies an in and out and done, right?"

He gave a soft groan. "Why is it that you say 'in and out' and I'm ready to go again?"

Wow, maybe she wasn't the only sex-starved one.

But that couldn't be right. Christopher could have any woman, she was sure of it. She didn't even know him, but the guy exuded sexy charm.

"We have to stop," she said. She resolutely pushed him back and pulled her bra straps up her arms. Because if he so much as said the word "nipple" to her, *she'd* be ready to go again.

Okay, she was already raring to go again. But she had *a few* of her wits.

He did pull his shirt over his head then. "You're right. Of course. Yeah. We do need to stop."

He didn't have to be quite *that* insistent.

"Right. This was a quickie. A one-time quickie," she said.

"Right. I'm leaving Sunday. This was a one-time thing."

He was leaving Sunday. Damn. That was three days away. Somehow she'd kind of liked the idea of running into him again, even if it was just for some flirting in the post office lobby or something. Then again, that was three days away. There was a lot they could do in three days...

She shook her head and stepped back. Or tried to. She was up against the door. The door she could open and leave through.

"Right. Okay. So..." She took a deep breath. "Thanks."

She'd never had a quickie, in a storeroom or otherwise, so she wasn't sure about the after-the-quickie etiquette.

"It was very nice to meet you, Regan," he said, humor obvious in his voice.

"Same. I hope you enjoy the rest of your stay in Bad." That was probably the stupidest thing she could have said, so it made sense that was what came out.

He chuckled at that. "I have a feeling the rest of the trip is going to have a hard time measuring up."

She laughed lightly too and felt warmth spread through her. Stupid. It wasn't as if he was really saying he'd enjoyed meeting and spending time with her. He'd enjoyed getting off.

Still, she liked the idea that he might think back on his trip and think of her.

"Okay, so, we maybe should go out separately?"

"I'm thinking anyone coming out of a storage closet might get noticed, but yeah, maybe."

And she didn't really want to be first. He was right. Going out there was going to attract attention, because who spent time in a storage closet?

"I'll go first," he said, moving close and nudging her out of the way.

She wanted him all over again. He'd put his arm against hers and she wanted him again.

Good grief.

He turned the knob. "And you might want to put your pants on before you come out."

He pulled the door open and stepped out, while she was blushing and scrambling to find her jeans.

By the time she had taken three times as long to pull on her jeans as she normally did, had gone through at least seven excuses as to why she had been in the storage closet if anyone asked, had taken three deep breaths and had finally opened the door, she went out—only to find no one was paying a bit of attention to her or even to this end of the building. Everyone had gathered around the front, where the bar stretched.

She ran her hand over her hair and casually made her way over to see why everyone was so interested in the horrible karaoke rendition of Billy Currington's "Pretty Good At Drinkin' Beer".

She came around the corner and froze.

Kurt was standing next to the jukebox, holding his fist to his mouth as if it was a microphone, belting out the lyrics.

With Christopher.

Christopher had his arm around Kurt and they were swaying and singing their hearts out.

Over the heads of their little fan club, Christopher saw her.

He gave her a smile and a wink.

And her heart tripped.

He was funny, charming, sexy, and damn, did he generously dish out the orgasms. And now he was creating a diversion so she could slip out of the closet.

Wow.

She made her way to the front door and pushed it open without anyone noticing. Except for the gorgeous guy with the deep green eyes whose gaze followed her out.

It was really too bad she was never going to see him again.

CHAPTER THREE

CHRISTOPHER BLEW out a breath and checked his watch.

He crossed an ankle over one knee. He checked his watch again. He reached for an old *Sports Illustrated* but didn't even open it. He rolled it up and tapped it against his shoe. He checked his watch again.

It was only five after ten. His appointment with the lawyer had been scheduled for ten. As a guy who had people waiting on him on a regular basis, Christopher knew that five minutes felt a lot longer on this side of the door. And that five minutes wasn't really all that long. But he was antsy.

It didn't help that he hadn't slept well the night before. He'd expected to feel completely comfortable, back in the little town he'd loved from the first minute he'd stepped onto Main Street. But comfortable was not how he would describe himself at the moment. Even though he was sitting in an office on Main Street in Bad.

Main Street Bad was a five-block stretch of quaint storefront businesses. And then there was The Bad Place, Dr. Patrick Faucheaux's long-time physical therapy practice. It was also on Main but was less 'quaint' and more 'you've got to be kidding'.

Rather than build a new modern clinic or restore one of the

buildings that had once been a hardware store or a butcher shop like all the other businesses along Main had done, Patrick had chosen a more...interesting building to turn into the physical therapy clinic.

He'd gotten a huge kick out of turning the old gaming parlor and brothel into a business called The Bad Place. Of course, it hadn't been a brothel in over a century, but it had been a casino. Then a jewelry store, then a bank, then a casino again up until the early eighties, when it became a department store that sold everything from clothing to hunting supplies to cookware. Then it had sat empty for about a decade before Patrick had bought it and turned it into his practice.

Not only did the main portion of the building still have twenty-two-foot ceilings with ornate plaster designs that were accented in gold, but there were matching plaster columns throughout the gigantic main space—also with decorative gold accents. Which went perfectly with the floor to ceiling mural of men and women in ancient Greek garb dancing and partaking of decadent food and drink. It was apparently written into all the legal paperwork around the building that the mural could not be painted over or the wall removed. Rumor had it that one of the women in the mural was painted to look like the original owner's wife, one was painted to look like his mistress, and one was painted to look like the woman he'd truly loved. No one knew which was which, but people had spent hours studying the mural and trying to decide.

In addition to the gaudy décor, there were other fabulous, dramatic stories that came with the building that made taking out the columns or changing the ceiling wrong somehow. There were ghost stories, murder and mayhem, wild affairs, and a jewelry heist that Christopher knew of.

Christopher had loved everything about it. People always smiled when inside the building, even when they were in pain and struggling. Everyone had a story or a theory about a story. And he loved the fact that patients showed up early for appointments because they might run into someone they knew in the waiting room and that would give them time for coffee and to chat.

But most of all, Christopher had loved how beloved Patrick had been. He'd been more than a physical therapist to this town. He'd been their counselor, their cheerleader, their confidant. He'd known everyone and seen them through their recoveries from accidents, sports injuries, illnesses, and aging. PTs had the opportunity to see clients from birth to old age and at every stage in between. They worked in multiple settings from schools to hospitals to outpatient clinics to patient homes to nursing homes. And Patrick had done it all in Bad and the surrounding area.

Patrick Faucheaux had been the kind of PT Christopher wanted to be. Strove to be.

Even when being that type of clinician was a huge disappointment to Christopher's parents, who had wanted him to be a big-city surgeon. Or, at least a small-city surgeon, like his father.

So coming back to Bad, to visit Patrick's grave, to retrieve whatever it was that Patrick had left him in his will, should have felt good. Sad and nostalgic, sure, but good.

And it had felt like coming home.

Until he met her.

Regan.

Regan, with the silky dark hair and big blue eyes and mischievous streak, who he'd had the hottest sex of his life with.

Regan, who had ruined all the comfortable, nostalgic feelings and filled him with heat and lust and need that had robbed him of several hours of sleep and was now making him antsy and edgy and distracted.

Because he wanted to find her.

He wanted another taste of her, but even more, he wanted to buy her coffee and get to know her.

In one night, *less than* one night, she'd turned the trip upside down and he felt a mix of guilt and desire that were at war inside him.

So far the guilt was winning, which was keeping him in the chair in the lawyer's office. For now. But the desire was building the longer he was awake, because the longer he was awake, the more minutes he spent replaying last night with her and every touch, every sigh, every pulse of pleasure.

He wanted more.

Christopher gripped the arms of his chair. Maybe it really was all the emotions of being back in Bad. Maybe it was the idea of truly facing the fact that Patrick was gone. He'd gotten to town around four the day before, so he hadn't really been here long. He'd purposefully avoided going past the clinic. He'd visited Patrick's grave, but Christopher knew that going to the clinic, and seeing it working without Patrick, would be when he missed his mentor the most, when it really hit that Patrick was gone.

Maybe all of that was working on his subconscious and making him feel more wound up than usual and he was attributing that to the night before with Regan.

That made more sense.

The door to the office opened and someone came in.

Christopher glanced up at the woman.

And froze.

It wasn't *a* woman.

It was *the* woman.

Regan.

And Christopher knew that no, his emotions about Patrick were not what had been driving him to go find her.

That was all her.

She wore denim capris, a yellow baseball cap, and a white t-shirt with bright yellow lettering that read *I'm Fine. It's Fine. Everything's FINE.* She looked like the typical girl next door. Any average woman about his age who he might pass on any side-walk in any city.

But his heart thumped hard and his body seemed to instantly strain toward her.

He straightened as she turned and came up short. "Oh." She frowned. "Hi."

He didn't know why, but he stood and faced her awkwardly. He hadn't felt awkward around a woman since he'd been twelve.

"Hi."

Regan looked around the waiting area. "What are you doing here?"

"I have a meeting with Mr. Benson."

"You do?"

"Yes."

"So do I."

Fate. That's what it had to be. What were the chances that they both had a meeting with the same lawyer and that one of them had gotten the time wrong? They were meant to see each other again.

"It's nice to see you," he told her. Completely honestly.

She blushed.

Christopher grinned. Ah yes, he knew exactly what memories were going through her mind. They were the same ones that had kept him awake much of the night.

"I'm…I didn't think I'd see you again," she said, her voice wobbly.

"Guess it's my lucky day."

The inner door swung open and a tall Black man came out. He gave them both a wide smile. "Good morning." He didn't seem surprised to see either of them.

Christopher stepped forward. "Mr. Benson. I'm Christopher Gilmore."

"Thank you for coming." Mr. Benson was in his fifties, with smile lines around his eyes and mouth and a little gray peppering his temples. His handshake was warm and firm.

Then he turned to Regan. "Good morning, Regan."

Christopher glanced at her. So she and the lawyer already knew one another.

She frowned. "What's going on?"

"We're going over the will," Mr. Benson said.

"Yes. Why is *he* here?" Regan asked, nodding toward Christopher.

The will? Regan was here about a will too? Wait, *the* will? Patrick's will?

"I need to speak with you both," Mr. Benson said calmly. He turned sideways and gestured toward his office. "Why don't we get started?"

Christopher was beyond curious at this point. He'd been wondering about his need to be here for two weeks, ever since Mr. Benson had called and asked him to come to Bad. This was the first time he'd been able to get to Louisiana from Nebraska, where he had been the sole practitioner in his clinic in Omaha while his business partner, Travis, was on paternity leave with his new daughter.

Of course, had he known this was more than a simple gift from an old friend, had he known he'd meet Regan, he would have closed the clinic and been on the plane the very next morning.

But what was Regan doing here? What did *this* have to do with her?

Christopher waited for Regan to pass in front of him.

It was clear that she kept her body stiff and carefully avoided brushing against him, but he still caught the whiff of buttercream. He took a deep, appreciative breath and he knew she noticed. She shot him a glare as she walked past.

Not exactly how he'd expected her to react when he saw her again. Or at least not how he'd *imagined* it. He hadn't expected it at all, but he'd let himself entertain a short fantasy about running into her again before he left town. The fantasy had caused him to spend a few more minutes in the shower than usual, easing the ache even the thought of Regan caused.

But glaring had not been a part of it.

At all.

Christopher followed her into the lawyer's office and took a seat in the chair next to the one she chose in front of the huge mahogany desk.

Mr. Benson took his chair, rested his forearms on the top of the desk and folded his hands.

"Thank you both for coming. Christopher, I appreciate you coming all this way. Regan, I appreciate your patience in getting this done."

Christopher glanced at Regan. She was here for Patrick's will reading as well. What were the chances of that? And why, even when he was preparing to hear his friend's final wishes, did he want to lean over and kiss her?

Regan didn't seem to be having any similar thoughts. Or really any positive thoughts at all. She was slumped in the chair, one leg crossed over the other, arms folded, looking pissy and pouty.

"I'm happy to be here," Christopher said, shifting on his chair to attempt to look open and casual to counteract Regan's obvious attitude.

"Let's just do this," Regan said.

Benson nodded and opened the folder in front of him. "There's no reason to do a formal reading of the will. Patrick just wanted me to be sure to talk with the two of you in person and together."

Christopher sat up a little straighter. Patrick had specifically requested that he and Regan be here together? What was going on? Why would she need to be here for him to receive the pocket watch or Patrick's old copy of *Huckleberry Finn* or his prized skeleton model that had hung in the corner of his office all his years in practice? Christopher had fully been expecting a sentimental token of their relationship as mentor and mentee. What did that have to do with Regan?

"As I told you on the phone, Christopher, Patrick had

suffered a TIA just prior to him coming in to update his will. He was afraid that something bigger was going to happen and he wanted to have everything in order."

Christopher had been surprised to hear of Patrick's TIA—transient ischemic attack—and his later stroke. A TIA was like a mini-stroke, and as a physical therapist, Patrick would have recognized how serious it was even if it cleared up within a few minutes. A TIA was a good predictor of a later stroke, and in Patrick's case, had been the precursor to a massive event that had killed him. Quickly. Benson had told Christopher that the TIA had been the first and only and had occurred just two weeks before the massive stroke that had killed his friend instantly.

Christopher's heart squeezed as he thought of his friend, knowing that the stroke was likely looming. There were things that could be done early in a stroke that could lessen the effects and improve outcomes afterward. In many cases. But not always.

He was, however, grateful that it had been fast and relatively painless.

"Regan, you and Christopher were his first priorities in getting things settled."

Christopher looked over at Regan again. Had she been one of Patrick's patients? Or one of his students as well?

"Are you a PT?" Christopher asked.

She sighed. "Yes."

He wasn't sure why he was surprised. Probably because it was something huge to have in common with the woman who had gotten under his skin so quickly. "You were one of Patrick's students too?"

She bit her bottom lip as she shook her head.

"Regan was Patrick's partner," Mr. Benson filled in.

Okay, the surprises kept coming. "Oh." Christopher frowned. "You must have just joined him in the past couple of years."

She blew out a breath. She still wasn't looking at him, but she said, "We were obviously in PT school at the same time. I was away while you were here. I came home to Bad knowing I wanted to work here with Patrick." Her voice broke on his name and she had to stop and swallow.

Christopher fisted his hand to keep from reaching for her.

"We'd talked for years about me becoming a PT and joining the practice with him."

"I...didn't know."

She blew out a breath. "I'm shocked he didn't talk about me." Her tone was dripping with sarcasm.

She looked as though she was fighting the urge to bolt. Her fingers dug into her arms, whitening her nails, and the look on her face was a mix of dread and anger.

What was going on?

"Shall I continue?" Mr. Benson asked.

"I told you before," she said tightly. "I'm not interested in any of it."

"Well, you have a couple of choices," Benson said. "You can decline your share of his estate and it will all go to Christopher. In which case, all physical property and assets become his."

"Great, let's do that." She shifted as if to stand.

Christopher was looking between the two of them. Estate? Assets? He'd been expecting a pocket watch.

He knew that Patrick had never married, choosing instead to dedicate his life to his work. It had been a conscious choice Patrick had made and he'd always seemed quite content with it. But Christopher had assumed there was a nephew or a cousin or a member of the community Patrick had served all these years that was closer to him and more important than Christopher.

Like Regan.

Christopher's heart thumped at that though. He'd had sex with Patrick's partner in a storeroom in a bar? He lifted his eyes to the ceiling and thought *Sorry, Patrick.*

"The assets include the clinic."

Regan froze.

"The entire business, not just the building," Benson said. "So if you give it all up, it will *all* go to Christopher solely."

Christopher and Regan *both* froze.

She looked at him and then they both looked at the lawyer.

"The whole thing?" she asked. "What about my half of the corporation?"

"Christopher will be given enough to buy you out."

Regan slumped back into her chair. "Damn him," she muttered.

Christopher frowned. "I really don't understand what's going on."

Mr. Benson gave Regan a questioning look.

"Go ahead and tell him," she said with a wave of her hand. "He's the only one in town who hasn't heard the whole sordid story."

Sordid story?

This morning was turning out a lot more interesting than he'd expected.

Mr. Benson looked over at Christopher. "As you know, Dr. Faucheaux was a beloved part of Bad for all of his life. He was like a brother, a father, a grandfather to many in this town."

Regan scoffed at that.

Christopher lifted an eyebrow at her but she refused to look at him.

Benson continued. "Patrick wanted to ensure that Regan had the *choice* to stay with the business. But he didn't want her saddled with it and stuck." He addressed Regan. "If you don't want it, he wanted there to be an easy and profitable way for you to get out of it. If you choose to give up your half, Christopher will have half a million dollars to use to buy you out."

She coughed slightly at the huge sum of money. "But Christopher doesn't get the choice to *not* be a partner here?" Regan asked.

"He has the same choice and you also have access to half a million dollars to buy him out if he doesn't want to stay."

Regan's eyes widened.

Christopher felt the shock vibrate through him. "I felt very close to Patrick," Christopher said. "And I'm touched. But I had no idea I was that important to *him*."

Benson nodded. "You and Regan are the only people named in his will. He has asked that some of his money and assets be divided among his charities, but you are the two that he specifically chose to carry out his last wishes and inherit what was most important to him—the practice."

Christopher didn't know what to say. He was touched beyond belief. He'd known that he and Patrick had a bond and that Patrick thought highly of him. He'd been choked up to know that Patrick had wanted him to have *anything*—a book, a watch or a skeleton. To know that he was one of two people Patrick thought of at the end...

One of two.

Christopher looked over at Regan. "What do you want to do? Obviously you were closer to him as his partner."

Regan gave a hard, humorless laugh. "Um, not exactly."

Mr. Benson filled in the blanks. "Regan is Patrick's daughter."

Regan felt the tears stinging her eyes and she cursed the man who had turned her life upside down a month ago.

Patrick Faucheaux. Dr. Patrick Faucheaux. One of her favorite people in the world. The guy who had always been the guy she'd *wished* could be her father. For a little girl without a dad and who'd been in a horrible car accident when she was only four, the man who had helped her walk again, who had eased her aches and pains, who always told her she looked pretty, and who had hung up the drawings she did for him by his desk and who always had her favorite bubblegum in his pocket, had been the guy she'd inserted into her daydreams about having a real family.

He had been about ten years older than her mother, but to a little girl, things like that didn't matter. He didn't have a wife or kids, he always smiled and laughed, and he made her feel safer than anyone else in the world. He had been her imaginary father for years.

They'd lived in another town until she'd been in fifth grade, but then her mom had moved them to Bad and Regan had been thrilled. She'd still had to do a lot of therapy, especially as she started playing more sports, so she'd seen Patrick more often as a patient, but also around town on a daily basis.

And then one day he'd called her and asked if she could come to his office. There, he'd told her the truth—that he and her mother had been in love at one time and she'd been the product. Then he'd asked her to lunch. As if he hadn't just changed her entire life.

They'd even stopped by to see one of his patients on their way to lunch. He was always, first and foremost, the PT to Bad.

Then they'd had turkey clubs at The Bad Egg and he'd told her how he hadn't known he was her father until the day her mother had taken Regan to see him because she was going to have another surgery on one of her legs. Her mother had asked if he'd give blood prior to the surgery because Regan shared his more rare type. She'd been sixteen. Which meant that he *had* known who she was for twelve years. And hadn't said anything.

Regan had been reeling from the shock of it all, trying to wrap her mind around it, trying to decide how she felt about it, what she wanted to do about it. He'd left that all up to her. He'd said their relationship could go on as it always had or he would leave her completely alone or he would be her father in every single way, every single day for the rest of his life.

She still hadn't decided what she wanted when, three days later, he'd died of a massive stroke.

He'd been right there and she'd been cheated of having a father, the perfect father in her mind, all of her life. She hadn't found out until there was no time left. Now she would never have all the answers, never know why he denied who he really was to her, never know why he wouldn't claim her as his own… and she'd never be able to hug him again, knowing that she did belong to someone.

Regan didn't feel the tear sliding down her cheek, until Christopher's finger touched her, wiping it away.

She jerked back and stared at him.

"I'm sorry, Regan," he said sincerely.

She wondered what he was sorry for. That she'd lost her father? That he'd fucked her in the storeroom last night not knowing who she was?

"I didn't know Patrick had a daughter." Christopher actually looked pained as he said it.

It was as if the idea bothered him. As if her identity would have made a difference…

Suddenly something clicked in her brain. "Oh my God, you're *Christopher*. Patrick's favorite student ever."

Christopher's eyebrows rose and a smile slowly spread his lips. "He talked to you about me?"

Yes. She'd gone to PT school because of Patrick and everything she'd gone through over the years as a patient herself. She'd ended up being a damned good athlete in spite of multiple broken bones, surgeries, pins and screws, and fucked up growth plates. She knew all about injury and rehab. It had seemed like a perfect fit.

Plus, her favorite person in the world was a PT.

She'd run into Patrick at a high school football game one weekend when she was home from PT school to visit. They'd sat together and talked throughout the game—about her studies and her internships, about the things she missed in Bad, about how he was doing and what was new in town. He'd not only mentioned Christopher, he'd *gushed* about Christopher. It had stuck with her because Patrick had been a mentor to numerous young physical therapists over the years, and she didn't remember ever hearing him talk that way about any of them. She specifically remembered Patrick saying that Christopher reminded him of himself when he'd been starting his career. She also remembered being very fucking jealous of Christopher. She'd always wanted to be Patrick's favorite.

Patrick Faucheaux had been beloved. He was a big-hearted, generous, warm man who had been totally devoted to his work. He'd lived it, breathed it, loved it. More than anything.

Which was why finding out she was his daughter hurt so much.

She'd known him. Her whole life. He'd taken care of her. He'd been there. He'd even made her his partner.

But that had just made sense. She was a hometown girl who'd gone and gotten a degree she could use in his clinic and she was the right age to take over the business after he retired.

She wasn't *Christopher* impressive to him.

She wasn't different or special.

She shook that off. Why did it matter? It didn't. Her life was no different now than it had been before she'd known. Not really. Yes, it hurt. But she'd spent twenty-eight years not knowing who her father was. It didn't change her life to know now. Especially since he was gone. It didn't matter.

But it really felt like it mattered.

Patrick had cared about her. He just hadn't cared more about her than he had anyone else. She'd grown up believing that her father hadn't cared enough about her to be around, so she wasn't sure why this was getting to her so badly.

Maybe because her father *had been* around. She just hadn't known it.

She was worried about her mental health, frankly.

"He talked about you," she finally told Christopher. "He loved you."

The words were like a sharp knife in her heart. He'd loved Christopher. Publicly, verbally, obviously. Like a son.

"I loved him too," Christopher said.

Though there was no way he could know the extent of her emotional turmoil, the way he studied her made Regan think he was seeing more than she wanted him to.

"I'm very sorry for your loss," he said softly.

But he had no idea what that loss really entailed.

"I had no idea that he had a child," Christopher said again. "He never—"

He stopped, but it was too late. Regan knew exactly what he had been about to say. Even if he *hadn't* started to say it. Patrick had never said a word about having a daughter.

"Yeah, well, I had no idea he had a daughter either," she said.

Christopher's brows pulled together. But he didn't say anything to that, just searched her eyes. After several long moments, he turned to the attorney. "What do you need from us?"

"A decision. But you have some time. Patrick also asked that you two be in charge of his personal and professional belongings. He wanted the two of you to actually go through his home and office. He said you are both welcome to keep anything you want, the rest he would like you to do with as you think best—donations, gifts, trash, whatever."

Regan felt her stomach knotting. Go through Patrick's stuff? Decide what to do with it all? How was any of that her problem or responsibility?

Christopher nodded, thoughtfully. "I'll probably need to take a little more time off."

"The timeline is that it be done in the next six months. It doesn't have to be right away," Mr. Benson said.

Regan pressed her folded arms against her stomach, but that certainly didn't make her feel *less* like throwing up. She got up from her chair, needing to move. She took a deep breath. "I can't do it." She looked from Mr. Benson to Christopher. "I'm sorry. We can hire someone to do it if you don't want to, or we can just open the place up and let whoever take whatever they want. I don't care."

Christopher didn't say anything to that, but he looked concerned.

Concerned for her? No. It couldn't be. They'd just met. He didn't really know her. There was no way he was actually feeling anything for her. Concerned about how big the job would be for him alone, probably.

"Your father—"

Regan cut Benson off. "Dr. Faucheaux. Or Patrick. He wasn't my father."

The attorney paused then said, "Patrick thought you might feel that way. He left this for you."

He held out a long cream-colored envelope.

A letter. From her dead father. Awesome.

She lifted her chin. "Not interested. I lived all my life without anything from him and I certainly don't need anything now."

Regan turned on her heel and headed for the door. She steeled herself for one of the men in the room to stop her.

She got the door open and even stepped through it, without anything from either of them.

Then she shut it behind her. Still with nothing.

Well, she should be used to that, she supposed. Nothing was exactly what she'd gotten from men all her life. This should be no different.

CHAPTER FOUR

CHRISTOPHER DIDN'T KNOW how to feel.

He was…spinning.

First, the news of Patrick's death, then the summons to Bad, then meeting Regan, and now all of this.

He wasn't sure what he was supposed to do. Or say. Or feel.

He leaned forward and put his elbows on his knees, dropping his head into his hands. This was a mess.

He'd slept with Patrick's daughter. Jesus, that was bad enough. Even if he hadn't known who she was. And what were the chances of that? Of all the women in Bad…

"Christopher."

He lifted his head and looked at Mr. Benson. "Yeah." He sat up in the chair. "Yeah, I'll do it. I can go through his office."

"And the other? Was Patrick right that you would be interested in the business?"

Christopher didn't have to think about that. "Yes. Strangely. My business in Omaha is only a little over a year old, but yes, I would consider coming here. I loved Bad when I was here before and I loved how Patrick practiced."

Back in Nebraska there were many small towns like Bad, but a city kid like Christopher couldn't just show up on Main

Street and start a business. Practices like Patrick's happened because someone *from* the town wanted to take care of the town.

Someone like Regan.

Christopher felt his heart squeeze. God, he hated what she was going through. What the hell had Patrick been thinking?

"Thank you. It meant a lot to Patrick to have the two of you here." Mr. Benson glanced at the door Regan had left through.

"What's the story with Regan?" Christopher asked. It wasn't really his business, and Benson might tell him that, but he couldn't keep from asking.

The older man sighed. "I don't know all of the details about why Patrick did or didn't do some of the things he did. I do know that he didn't know Regan was his until about twelve years ago. I don't know all of Patrick's thought processes behind not telling her, though. I also know that he was incredibly proud of her and tried to be as close to her as he could."

Christopher knew he was about to wade waist deep into something that was none of his business and something that he wasn't so sure he could fix. But that didn't matter. Patrick mattered to him and, for some crazy reason, Regan did too.

Sure, the sex had been awesome. Yes, he'd like to do it again. And maybe it was *because* she was Patrick's daughter. Maybe that made him want to get to know her better.

Christopher stretched to his feet. "Let me talk to her."

Mr. Benson nodded. "Thank you."

He handed over a set of keys Christopher assumed were for the clinic and the apartment above the clinic where Patrick had lived, along with two envelopes. One was the letter from Patrick to Regan. The other had his name on the front.

"He wrote one to you too," Mr. Benson said.

Christopher swallowed hard at that. "Um, thanks."

"Let me know if you need anything else. Also when you leave town, okay?" the lawyer asked.

Christopher nodded. "I won't be leaving anytime soon.

There's a lot to take care of here." He knew that without even knowing the state of Patrick's office.

Mr. Benson inclined his head in agreement. "Let me know if I can be of any assistance."

"Thanks."

Christopher pocketed the keys and folded the two envelopes together, tucking them into his back pocket. The first thing he wanted to do was find Regan.

He turned back. "You wouldn't have any idea where Regan might go?"

Mr. Benson shook his head. "I'm sorry, not for sure. You could try The Bad Egg just down the street—they do have awesome hot fudge sundaes." He smiled. "Or there's Bad Brews. One of her best girlfriends works at City Hall. Another is one of our mechanics at Bad Brakes. But Bad isn't very big."

For some crazy reason, Christopher was glad to know that Regan had friends and that she would likely go to them when she was sad and mixed up. If she didn't go for ice cream or booze, of course. "Thanks."

Christopher stepped out onto the wooden sidewalk and took a deep breath. He looked up and down the street. Where to start?

He felt the envelopes shifting in his back pocket and made a decision. He was going to stop by the clinic first. Maybe she went there. It was partially hers after all. And if she wasn't there, maybe seeing that alone the first time would be good. He was prepared to feel emotional about it one way or another, but he didn't hate the idea of *not* showing that side to Regan. Maybe because the man he was going to be emotional over was causing some pretty strong emotions for her too—and none were positive.

Christopher thought about that as he headed up the street. That was bugging him, he could admit. Regan was upset, angry even, at a man Christopher loved.

Christopher's own father, a surgeon, had been a distant man, consumed by his work. Christopher had initially expressed interest in medicine when his mom had been diagnosed with diabetes when he was in high school. His father had scoffed. He'd told him he was too softhearted to be a good physician. Christopher had taken his initial pre-med classes in college simply as a *fuck you* to his dad. Don Gilmore loved telling people what they could and couldn't do. Christopher had decided he was done with that the minute he'd moved out. If he wanted to be a doctor, he'd be a doctor. And a damned good one.

He'd flown through his pre-med classes and loved every minute of them. Then he'd blown out his ACL playing a pick-up game of basketball and had ended up in PT himself and had realized *that* was what he wanted to do with his life. That had been a relief. Christopher had almost regretted how much he loved medicine, wanting to have less in common with Don rather than more. When he'd experienced how different, how personal physical therapy was, he understood that they might both have Dr. in front of their names, but that and a few pieces of DNA were all they shared.

And then he'd met Patrick Faucheaux and Christopher had found someone he could look up to and emulate in all he did. There had even been a couple of moments where Christopher had wished Patrick could have been his father instead.

He turned the corner that would lead him to the clinic and shuddered a little. Now that he'd had sex with Patrick's *actual* child, the idea of Patrick being *his* father was a little...disturbing.

Christopher approached the back of the clinic and saw that someone was sitting on the steps that led up to the second floor where Patrick had lived. Someone with a bright yellow cap.

Okay, well, he'd found her.

He walked up the sidewalk and stopped. Regan was sitting on the fourth step.

"I decided that you shouldn't have to do this all yourself," she said.

"Was it the half a million dollars or the orgasms that made you so concerned about me doing this job alone?" he asked.

She grimaced.

And he felt like an ass.

He hadn't meant to be sharp with her, but evidently her having an intense dislike for her father, the man Christopher had wished could have been *his* father—other than the sleeping-with-Patrick's-real-daughter thing—had made him edgy.

He took a breath. "Sorry. I'm glad you're here. I was going to come and find you."

That was better.

She cocked an eyebrow. "Was it the idea of doing this huge cleanup job alone or the orgasm that made you so concerned about finding me?"

Okay, he deserved that.

He tipped his head to the side and studied her. What was it about this woman?

"I'm thinking it must be the orgasm," he finally said. He really wasn't sure what else it could be. He'd just met her and didn't really know her. And what he did know was that they shared very opposite feelings for Patrick Faucheaux. "I was pretty close to coming to find you even before I knew about the cleanup job."

Her eyes widened and her cheeks got a tiny bit pink. "You were?"

"I've been thinking about you nonstop and the fact that I'm here for three more days and how much fun we could have in that time." He looked up at the house. "And now I'm here for more than three days." He focused on her again. "And now we're kind of stuck together."

She wet her lips.

Being stuck together with her seemed like one of the best things to happen to him in a long time.

Regan got to her feet. "I will go through his apartment

upstairs and you can go through his office. We'll see...how we feel after that."

Christopher stepped up two steps, putting him closer and more on level with her. "Are you expecting your feelings for me to change?"

"Wanting to sleep with you? No," she said, honestly, meeting his eyes. "But, contrary to how it probably seemed last night, if it's more than a storeroom quickie, I probably need to like you a little bit. And I have a feeling we're going to go inside this house and you're going to try to get me to feel differently about Patrick than I do right now. And if you do that, I'm probably not going to like you. Which means, I probably won't sleep with you again."

He thought about her words. She was right. He had been subconsciously entertaining ideas of helping her through her negative feelings about Patrick. Whether that was about his feelings for Patrick or for her, he wasn't sure.

"Probably," he finally said.

"What?"

"You said you're *probably* not going to like me and *probably* won't sleep with me again."

"Right."

"Probably isn't a for sure."

She sighed. "So it's going to be like that? We're going to go in there, go through his stuff, you're going to try to convince me to forgive him and you're also going to try to convince me to have sex with you again."

Christopher thought that through as well. Then nodded. "Yep. Pretty much."

"Awesome." She eyed the sidewalk behind him, clearly contemplating an escape.

"Hey, half a million dollars—or a PT practice—and another dozen orgasms isn't a bad deal, is it?" he asked, really not wanting her to escape at all.

She focused on his eyes again. "Another dozen?"

"I can do even more, but we do have a cleanup job to do. You'll have to explain to Benson what's taking so long."

Christopher hadn't realized how tensely he'd been holding himself until she laughed and the tightness flowed out of him.

Regan smiled at him for a moment then slowly the smile faded. "I want to keep the practice. I'm ninety-percent sure. But that's not why I'm doing this."

"I'm not judging."

"But… I don't know why I'm doing this."

"Maybe you want to get to know him better?" Christopher suggested.

Regan shook her head, dropping her gaze to the step she stood on and pushing her hands into the pockets of her pants. "I knew him. Really well. He's been around all my life. He helped me walk again after my car accident. He's been a part of this town for as long as I can remember. I've always…"

Her voice caught for a moment and Christopher had to make himself stay put on the step rather than grabbing her.

She sniffed. "I've always loved him."

Christopher felt a huge wave of relief at that. She didn't hate his mentor and friend. She didn't really want to never speak of him again. She was hurt. She was grieving for someone she loved and she'd just found out a huge secret about him. And about herself.

"For what it's worth," Christopher said gently, "I understand. And I meant it about not judging."

She sniffed again and nodded. "Thanks."

"Maybe you want to do this for the same reason I do," Christopher said. "Just because he asked me to."

She lifted her head.

"I had no idea why Patrick wanted me to come back to Bad when I said yes, but I did it because he wanted me to. I guess I'm here and doing this because of all the things he did for me."

She nodded slowly. "Yeah, maybe that's it." She took a deep breath and stood straighter. "Actually, that is it. I always felt like maybe I was a little special to him. He was always kind and sweet with all the kids—heck, all of the *people*—in this town. But there was something that always made me feel like...I don't know...maybe like I was his favorite." She gave him a sheepish grimace. "I might have made that all up in my mind. Because when he told me that I was his daugh..." She tripped over the word. "...daughter, I started feeling like I wasn't special at all. He kept that from me. He never once acted like there was anything *more* between us. Until it was too late. And that hurt. But then today, when I found out that he only named the two of us..." She took a deep breath and met Christopher's eyes directly. "I know how he felt about *you*, and thinking that he'd put me in there with you made me think that maybe I meant a little something more to him."

Christopher couldn't stay on his step any longer. He moved up to stand right in front of her on her step. He took her face between his hands simply because he couldn't *not* do that. "There's no way you weren't special to him," he said. "I knew Patrick. I worked side by side with him, watched him, learned from him. He was good at so many things, but nothing more than loving people. There is no way he didn't love you. There had to be a reason he never told you who he was."

She was staring up at him as if startled. Whether it was the way he'd just invaded her personal space or what he'd said or the emotion behind his words, which frankly startled *him* a little too, he wasn't sure. But her big blue eyes were definitely startled.

Not that Christopher let go of her or stepped back.

Oh, no. In fact, those eyes made him move in even closer.

She sucked in a little breath and her lips parted.

And for that moment, he completely forgot why he was there, who she was, what he was *supposed* to be doing, and he lowered his head, capturing her lips in a soft, sweet kiss that seemed to wrap around his heart and a body part a lot lower at the same time.

When he lifted his head, she was breathing faster.

"I really want to help you with this," he said.

"Why?" she asked softly.

Good question. "I'm not sure. It's…kind of who I am."

She took a breath and stepped back. He let her go.

For now. That was all he could think.

"That's who you are. That makes sense," she said with a shaky little smile.

"It does?"

"It's who he was too. The protector. The fixer. The guy who wanted to always make everything better."

Christopher couldn't deny it. Those were things he was proud of, actually. He nodded. "Yeah. That's who I am."

"And that's why he wanted us to hear all of that together."

That idea shot…something…through Christopher. "You think he wanted me here when you heard everything?"

She shrugged. "Yeah. I do. I think he knew that you'd want to help me through it."

That made Christopher feel, well, a whole lot of complicated things. "So, see? He knew this would be tough on you and he wanted to make it as easy as he could," Christopher finally said.

"Yeah, I guess so."

"That shows he cared about you."

"Yeah."

She didn't look totally convinced, but she didn't need to be. "I know you have a lot of questions, Regan," Christopher said. "So let's go in and see if we can find some answers."

She looked over at the door. "I guess I do have a few."

"And you want to do his apartment? The more personal stuff?" he clarified.

She nodded. "I worked with him every day for the past three years." Her voice was a little wobbly when she said it. "I didn't nose around in his office, but I feel like I know that side of him pretty well. I think I want to see if there's more to his personal side that I didn't know."

Christopher remembered the letters then. He pulled the envelopes from his pocket. "Here. This might help too."

She looked like he was trying to hand her a poisonous snake. "I don't know." She shook her head. "I'm not sure I'm ready for that."

Christopher pulled the letter back. "Okay. Well, I have one too. I'll hang on to yours until you're ready to see it."

"Are you going to read yours?"

"Yes. For sure."

She took a breath and then stuck her hand out. "Okay. Give me mine. I'll see if I can work up the guts."

He smiled as he gave it to her. "Let me know if you need me to hold your hand while you read it."

She looked from the envelope to his face. "What if I need a kiss later to make it all better?"

He liked her, he wanted her, he felt strangely protective of her, and he *loved* her flirty side. He grinned. "Absolutely. I'm here for you."

Regan gave a light laugh and he felt as if he'd accomplished a lot.

"Thanks. I appreciate that." She turned and faced the front door.

He moved in beside her and pulled the keys from his pocket. "Ready?"

"Nope."

"We going in anyway?" he asked.

"Yep."

Yeah, he definitely liked her.

Two hours later, Regan sat on the floor in the middle of the living room area in the upstairs apartment, surrounded by books and boxes.

It was one thing to go through Patrick's kitchen and pack up dishes. That wasn't so bad. His closet and dresser, sorting through clothes and shoes she recognized had been a little harder. But it was a whole new ballgame to go through photos and notebooks and letters.

She still hadn't read her letter from him. But she'd read about twenty that he'd received from other people. And that was a very, very small dent in the huge pile of letters Patrick had kept over the years.

It didn't surprise her that he'd kept them once she started reading. They were letters from patients. People he'd helped, people he'd gone the extra mile for. Not that he didn't always do that. These were just the people who'd thought to write and tell him what he meant to them.

She finished the third one, from a mother who was thanking Patrick for his help with her child's serious illness. Regan dropped the letter to her lap and sighed. She looked around.

She was going through his personal things but there was a lot of his professional life here.

Not just the letters. Mixed amongst the fiction novels and magazines were texts and journals. The entertainment center that held an old TV and stereo had shelves full of records, cassette tapes and CDs, everything from Frank Sinatra to, surprisingly, Justin Timberlake. But between piles of tapes and CDs, he also had rolls of athletic tape, packages of gauze, bottles of ibuprofen, and ten boxes of business cards. Patrick had never needed to hand out business cards. Everyone knew who he was and how to find him. It was no wonder all the cards were still in his apartment.

He had photos everywhere, and there were as many taken with people in the hospital or nursing home or with casts and braces on various body parts as there were with friends and neighbors. Then again, those patients had been his friends and neighbors.

Of course there were no photos of family. Patrick hadn't had a family. He'd been raised in Bad, but his parents had died a long time ago and he didn't have brothers or sisters. He'd never married nor had kids.

Well… Regan faltered there. He had. Obviously. One.

At least.

The sudden thought hit her—did he have other children? Ones he knew about? Ones he didn't? Did she have half siblings?

Did she *know* any of them?

She'd always wanted brothers and sisters. Lots of them.

She'd had a lot of friends and she'd never felt lonely exactly. But she had seen what other kids had—a mom and dad, brothers and sisters, family vacations, big Christmas dinners.

It had always been just her mom and her. And her mom had never been up for vacations and big dinners.

Nancy Reynolds had been diagnosed with bipolar disorder about a year before Regan had been born. Her mother's ups and downs had always been a part of her life. That hadn't made it easier, exactly, but Regan hadn't known any different.

Nancy had confided once, when Regan was an adult herself, that she had planned to not have children after her diagnosis, because she'd been certain her own mother had also suffered from the condition but had gone undiagnosed. It had made Nancy's life very hard. She hadn't wanted to pass the condition on to a child of her own.

And then Regan had come along.

Nancy had been pretty consistent with her medications and treatments. She'd done what she could to manage things. But it had been tough. The treatments hadn't always worked. Or they hadn't worked enough.

It was the reason Nancy had never married, either. She had seen how miserable her mother had made her father and had vowed to never do that to someone.

It had all struck Regan as very sad, but she respected her mother making decisions with other people in mind, even if her fears had kept Regan from having a family.

She remembered telling her mom that Patrick had died. Nancy's reaction had been to nod and to head straight to bed.

After Regan had found out who Patrick really was, she'd confronted Nancy. But she'd quickly backed down. Her mother's emotional state had always been tenuous. Regan tiptoed around her mother as she always had. Not upsetting Nancy had become Regan's primary goal. When her mother had gotten agitated about Regan's newfound knowledge about her father, Regan had assured her that she wasn't angry and that she was happy to know who he was.

Regan pushed herself up from the floor, her back and legs stiff from sitting for so long. She paced across the apartment, scanning all the other things that needed "going through". She assumed that going through Patrick's apartment meant going through *everything* in the place. Mr. Benson had said to keep, donate or trash what she found. This could take forever. Patrick wasn't quite to hoarder status but his bookshelves were nearly busting at the seams.

She crossed to the bookcase that took up one entire wall.

Again, there were fiction novels by the dozens, but there were plenty of medical texts, anatomy books and such. There was even one with his name on the spine.

Patrick had written a book?

She pulled the volume from the shelf.

The Art of Healing.

Something about the title, and the fact that he'd written a book, made Regan smile.

No matter her feelings about Patrick's contribution to her DNA, she'd always known he was an amazing physical therapist. He'd lived for it. It was his life.

She glanced around the room. Maybe that's why there were so many pieces of his work here in his living space. His work was his life, and his life was his work.

Regan flipped open the cover of the book and started turning pages. The pages seemed to automatically flip to one where several photographs were tucked.

It took her a moment to realize what she was seeing.

In the pages of the book that Patrick Faucheaux had written about his one and only love and passion, he had tucked photos of Regan's mother.

Nancy was young in the photos, surely not more than in her early twenties, but there was no mistaking that it was her. In fact, Regan looked a lot like her.

There were five pictures in all. One was of Nancy leaning against a tree, smiling at the photographer. The next was of her swinging on a swing. She was in the same outfit so Regan assumed it was the same day and they were at a park. There was another picture of her on the swing but this one was closer up, showing more of her face, the obvious sparkle in her eye and the huge smile. And finally, two photos of her lying in the grass on a blanket. One was, again, from farther back, a happy smile, one that Regan hadn't seen very often in her life, firmly in place. And then the final photo, the one that took Regan's breath. Nancy was still lying on the blanket, but this up-close photo showed a softer smile, one that went perfectly with the look in her eyes. It was the look of love.

Her mother had clearly loved whoever was behind the camera.

With her hand against her mouth, Regan turned the photo over.

Me and Nancy, July.

Me. Was the me Patrick? It almost had to be, didn't it? Why would he have photos like this that someone else had taken?

Regan looked at her mom's face again. Happy. So happy. Regan hadn't seen that enough over the years. Nancy's up periods were more common than her down, but even they were tempered by medication and, as Regan had learned later, fear. Fear of what she would do during her euphoria if it got out of hand.

If Nancy was around twenty or twenty-one in the photos, that meant they were taken four or five years before Regan had been born. If this was Patrick, that meant her mother and father had had a relationship. Even if it had been on again/off again, it had gone on for a little while.

"Hey."

Though the greeting was soft, it made Regan jump.

"Sorry, didn't mean to scare you." Christopher came farther into the living room. "I said your name but you didn't hear me."

She took a deep breath. "Sorry. I was lost in thought."

"Seemed so," he said with a nod. "Good thoughts?"

She looked down at the photo. Yeah, mostly good. And suddenly she wanted to talk about it.

With Christopher.

That was the strange part. She had girlfriends she could go to. Randi and Priscilla both knew about Patrick and that she'd had the meeting with the lawyer scheduled today and were no doubt dying to know how it had gone. But she hadn't called them yet. She'd thought about it. She'd thought about calling and spilling her guts about the sexy stranger she'd gotten naughty with at the Bad Brews too.

But she hadn't done that either.

Why not? This was exactly the kind of thing they told each other.

But now, looking back up at Christopher, she knew. She wanted to keep him to herself for a while. And like it or not, this whole thing with Patrick included Christopher.

Though she was starting to think she liked it.

CHAPTER FIVE

REGAN TURNED the picture of her mom on the swing so he could see it.

"This is my mom."

Christopher crossed the room and Regan felt her heartrate accelerating as he came closer.

Just walking across the room he could make her get all tingly. Dang.

He took the photo from her fingers and studied it. "You look just like her," he said, lifting his gaze to Regan's. "She's very beautiful."

Regan flushed slightly but rolled her eyes. "You already got lucky, Doc. No need to butter me up."

He gave her a grin and handed the photo back. "I already got lucky *once*. And I can do better than a simple—not to mention indirect—compliment if I'm worried about the second time."

Something about the way he said that made her pretty sure he wasn't at all worried about the second time.

Nor should he be.

He was just standing there and her whole body seemed to be already priming for his touch, his kiss…everything.

"You can do better than a simple indirect compliment?" she asked.

He moved in closer, just as she'd hoped, and lifted his hand to her face, just as she'd hoped.

"Oh yeah. Something like this, for instance." He stroked the pad of his thumb over her bottom lip.

Heat spread through her from that one small point of contact and her lips parted. She couldn't help it. That thumb stroke reminded her of several from the night before.

"Or this." He ran all of his fingertips down the side of her throat.

The action caused goose bumps to trip down her arm and chest and her nipples to bead.

Damn. How did he know that was going to happen?

His gaze followed as he ran his hand down over the V neckline of her shirt and over the side of her breast. Her nipples puckered tighter and she knew he noticed. Her soft cotton bra and t-shirt weren't enough to hide her reaction. He dragged his thumb over one stiff tip like he had over her lip.

But the thing that rocked her hardest, made her want him badly, was the way he caught her gaze with his as he did it. He didn't look at her nipple or the rest of her body for pleasure or to gauge her reaction to his touch. He looked into her eyes.

She was sure they told him everything he needed to know. She felt as if she was practically glowing with lust.

And he'd touched her lip, neck and one nipple.

"But this isn't why I came up here," he said, dropping his hand.

The sudden lack of contact and, well, seduction threw her.

She blinked at him stupidly for a few beats.

"I found something I think you should see."

Regan pulled herself together and wet her lips. Something she should see. From downstairs. In Patrick's office. Patrick. Right. The apartment. The will.

"Okay," she said.

Christopher gave her a knowing grin and she hated for a second that he could affect her so easily, and that he knew it.

"I think you should look at this." He held up what appeared to be a scrapbook.

She frowned. "Okay."

They headed for the couch and sat down side by side.

"And here. I think you should have this." She handed him Patrick's book.

Christopher took it and ran a hand over the cover. "You don't want it?"

"I got to practice right beside him for three years. I got to see that book happening in real life. I want you to feel as close to him as you can and that book is probably it."

Christopher looked genuinely touched. "Thank you."

She tipped her head, watching him. "You already have a copy don't you?" She wasn't sure how she knew, but she did.

He smiled at her and nodded. "Yes. But this was his personal copy. I will cherish this and I'll pass my copy on to my mentee someday."

"You have a mentee?" she asked. "Never mind. Of course you do."

He chuckled. "I don't, actually. Not yet."

"Huh. You totally seem the type to be a mentor."

"You don't know me that well," he said. But Regan could tell that he took it as a compliment.

"No, but..." Her gaze fell on Patrick's book again. "I knew *him*. And if you admire him, it makes sense you'd want to be like him and if you want to be like him, that means teaching. All the time. It was one of the things he loved best."

Christopher nodded. "It was. And thank you for letting me go through his office. I feel closer to him because of that too. I'm learning some things."

"I'm glad. Me too, being up here. Even though I've known him all my life."

"As your PT."

"And friend. He loved this town and he was always around, at everything. He came to plays and recitals and ballgames and programs. He was always in the audience." She was holding the photos of her mother, her gaze on the up-close photo of her in the grass. Was it possible that he had been showing up to see her specifically? Or even to see her mother?

"Wow." Christopher reached for the photo.

"She looks really in love and happy doesn't she?" Regan asked.

"She really does." He looked up at her. "I can see why Patrick kept that one in a special place."

"Yeah?"

He nodded. "That look on her face in the photo—that takes her from beautiful to stunning."

Regan saw the love shining in Nancy's eyes, but she liked knowing that Christopher was seeing the same thing.

"Oh yeah," Christopher said, handing it back. "Every guy wants to be looked at like that by the woman he loves."

His words hit Regan square in the chest. "Looked at like what?"

"With that—" Christopher pointed to the picture. "That combination of love and lust."

Regan stared at the photo. Lust? But yeah, now that he mentioned it…

"That was the last photo he took that day. The others came before that one," Christopher said.

"How do you know?"

"Because with that look on her face, they had other things to do after that."

He gave her a grin that made her toes curl.

"So you do think Patrick took these photos?"

Christopher looked surprised. "Don't you?"

"I…hope so."

His expression gentled. "You want to know that your parents were in love. Even if it was briefly."

She wasn't sure why she wasn't more surprised that he'd figured that out about her. She nodded. "Every child wants that, right?"

"Definitely." He looked at the photo again. "And absolutely Patrick took that picture."

"Yeah?" She peered at it, wondering what he saw to make him so sure.

"There's no way I'd keep a picture of a woman looking at another guy like that. Unless I was a masochist. And there's no way Patrick was a masochist. He was way too loving and self-accepting."

He was right.

She sighed. "Thanks."

"For what?"

"Making me feel better. I don't think anyone else in town knew him like you and I did. Sharing his professional passion helps us understand him differently, I think. It means a lot when you say that kind of stuff because you actually know."

"Well, you're welcome." He bumped her shoulder with his. "Now look at what I brought you."

Regan felt a sense of trepidation steal over her as she opened the scrapbook.

And rightly so, she discovered a moment later.

Her eyes flew up to Christopher's. He nodded. "Amazing right?"

That was not the word she'd been searching for.

The first page of the scrapbook was a photo that she had seen thousands of times in her life. It had hung on the wall in the living room of the house she'd grown up in for as long as she could remember.

It was her baby picture.

She couldn't come up with any words to use, so she flipped the page. Another photo of her, this one on the first day of fourth grade. She had her backpack on and a huge grin, she was holding her Powerpuff Girls lunchbox.

She missed the Powerpuff Girls.

"That's you right?" he asked.

She nodded, flipping the next page. More pictures of her. A program from her second grade school music program.

She looked up. "Patrick didn't know about me until I was sixteen. This doesn't make sense."

"Your mom gave him stuff after she told him? To try to make up for all the years he'd missed?" Christopher suggested.

She kept turning pages. "Yeah, maybe."

As she got farther back in the book, there were still photos but there were also coloring book pages and drawings. From her.

"I remember giving him things I'd made," she said softly, looking at the penguin and polar bear she'd colored in. The polar bear was green and the penguin purple, their scarves red and their boots blue. Above their heads someone had written To Dr. Patrick From Regan. It was clearly her mother's handwriting and Regan shook her head. "I don't get it. They obviously had some feelings for one another at one time."

"And he obviously had some feelings for you," Christopher said gently. "Even if he didn't know you were his daughter back when you drew those, he kept them anyway."

She nodded. "Probably no one else drew as many for him." She laughed. "I was always drawing and coloring."

"Do you still draw?"

She looked up at him. It felt so strange that he didn't know the answer to that question, but she reminded herself that she'd known him for less than twenty-four hours. That was so weird because she felt so close to him.

She gave him a little grin. "I do."

His return smile made her chest feel warmer for some reason. "I'm very glad to hear that."

And he sincerely seemed glad. Which was strange as well.

"Yeah?" she asked him. "You've always wanted to do it with an artist in a storeroom at a bar?"

He leaned in, the look in his eyes hot…and promising. "Turns out, yes. Without even knowing it."

Okay, that was pretty sweet.

"Thank you for bringing this up," she said of the scrapbook.

"I'm glad it turned out to be a good thing."

"Because you really want me to not hate Patrick?"

He lifted his hand and did that thumb on her lip thing again. "A few hours ago, I would have said yes. Now…"

She really wanted to hear the rest of that. "Now?"

"Now I think I'm willing to do just about anything that makes you smile."

Oh boy. Sweet. And hot. And…trouble.

Mind back on Patrick. Focus. You're here for a reason other than the hot guy next to you.

"I miss him."

Christopher paused and then leaned back slightly. "I do too."

"And, honestly, I don't hate him. I never did. But I was mad. And I still am."

"Have you read your letter yet?" he asked.

She had almost forgotten about the letter.

"No." But she wanted to now more than she had a few hours ago. "You?"

"Yep."

She wasn't surprised. "Was it good?" She wanted to know what was in it. "Never mind, none of my business." It wasn't, but it felt like it was. Also strange.

"Actually, it kind of is." Christopher leaned to one side and reached into the back pocket of his jeans, pulling out the folded envelope.

"It's kind of my business what Patrick wrote to you in that letter?" Regan asked.

"Yeah. You want to read it?"

She looked at the envelope. She saw the handwriting on the front and her heart twinged. She'd seen Patrick's handwriting hundreds of times over the years, but she hadn't realized it would make her miss him so much.

"Do I want to read it?" she asked. She knew Christopher would give her an honest answer about that. For some reason she felt like he...cared

That was stupid, of course. He didn't even know her.

"I think it's interesting. It might make you want to read yours," he said honestly. "It made *me* want to read yours."

Okay yeah, she was interested. She held out her hand and Christopher laid the envelope in it.

With a deep breath, she slid the single piece of paper inside of it out and unfolded it.

Dear Christopher,

Looking back, I realize that I did, in fact, say the things I wanted to while you were here—I'm proud of you, you will be an amazing PT who will have a long and rewarding career, you have found something that all people unknowingly wish for—a way to spend your life doing something that you love. You have passion, you have heart, you have intelligence, you have humor. I'm proud to call you more than a student of mine...I'm proud to call you my friend.

But you know all of that.

You also know that I would love nothing more than for you to take over my practice and care for the people I've loved and lived amongst all my life.

It's a lot to ask, I realize. I promise not to haunt you if you choose not to, but do consider it. Not only will they be in good hands, but so will you.

But there's more. A favor I've intended to ask you for a long time now.

I was waiting for the right moment, but the right moment has come to me—and sooner than I expected.

The favor is this—I want you to get to know my daughter.

That's all. Get to know her. Not as a possible business partner, but as a person. Talk for a little while. Listen to her laugh. Let her tell you about her patients. Watch her with her friends. Ask her about her mom.

Regan doesn't know it all the time, but she is amazing. I have loved her from the moment I met her, which was the first time she needed stitches. I didn't know she was my daughter for years. But I didn't need to. I loved her because of who she was all on her own.

Much as I loved you from when we first met.

You share my love and passion for everything else. It's my hope that you will love her as much.

I realize this is a crazy thing to write. I realize that I have no right to ask this. I realize that this isn't generally how the universe and falling in love work.

But by the time you read this, I'll be gone and you can go ahead and think I'm crazy all you want.

But I know you. If it isn't everything I hope it is, then at least I'll know that you'll both have a lifelong friend who shares a professional passion and also has some fond memories of me.

Patrick

It was clear that Regan was having a hard time fighting the tears. Her hand covered her mouth and she continued to blink down at the handwritten page long after she should have been done reading it.

Christopher just sat and waited.

What was he really going to say, anyway? Patrick had wanted them to meet. Fate had made that happen in the bar last night, but Patrick had brought Christopher back to Bad.

Hell, he was having a hard time fighting his emotions about all of this too.

It was crazy that Patrick had thought Christopher could fall for Regan.

But as soon as he thought it, he wondered *why* that was crazy. Patrick knew them both very well. He had loved them both. It wasn't *crazy* that he would think they might hit it off.

People played matchmaker all the time. People set their

friends up on blind dates or invited single friends to dinner parties with the intention of having them meet another single friend.

This actually wasn't all that crazy.

Finally Regan looked up at him, her eyes shiny with tears. "So, now what?"

Now what? Indeed. A great question.

Proposing seemed like a leap. Asking her take her clothes off was maybe inappropriate at the moment. "We could read your letter."

She nodded. "Yeah, okay." She rose and crossed to a little space on the floor that was surrounded by boxes, as if she'd built a fort. She bent and picked up the envelope that matched his.

With a deep breath, she pulled out the letter.

But she didn't unfold it. She turned to him. "Would you read it first?"

"You sure?"

She nodded and came toward him. She handed it over.

Christopher opened the letter and started reading.

Dear Regan,

You have been the light in my life as long as I've known you.

I remember the day I found out that you were my daughter. It wasn't as much a shock as I might have expected. It seemed right. It seemed, in some ways, that I'd known somewhere deep down all along.

Christopher looked up. "Do you want me to read this out loud?"

Regan crossed her arms and pressed them against her stomach. She looked nervous. But something more...hopeful. "I don't know. Do I?"

Christopher gave her an encouraging smile. "I think so."

She nodded. "Okay."

He started over. "Dear Regan, You have been the light in my life as long as I've known you. I remember the day I found out that you were my daughter. It wasn't as much a shock as I might have expected. It seemed right. It seemed, in some ways, that I'd known somewhere deep down all along."

Christopher glanced up. A single tear tracked down her face. But she said softly, "Go on."

He cleared his throat and continued. "I know you're wondering why—why would your mother keep you from me, why would I not tell you what I knew after I found out? It's hard to explain, but I'll try. Neither your mother nor I wanted to get married. We knew that from the beginning. We fell in love, we enjoyed each other, and we thought that we could keep on with an affair only forever. It wouldn't have hurt anyone. We never intended to get involved with anyone else and we never intended to have children. Seeing each other every couple of weeks for short periods worked well for us. I was so consumed with work, and that's how I wanted to be. Your mother was dealing with her condition and short term was the only thing she could give."

Christopher felt his stomach knotting and he looked up again.

Regan's eyes were still watery and she hadn't moved a muscle. But her face looked less fearful and more pained now.

"You sure?" he asked gently.

She nodded.

He took a breath and kept going. "Then you came along. I didn't know until your mother was nearly seven months pregnant. She simply kept saying she couldn't see me and I listened. That was how we had agreed to do things. When I did finally see her, she told me that we had to break things off. In my hurt and shock, I believed that she'd been with someone else. We stopped speaking and seeing each other. I hadn't realized until then, how much I'd loved her.

"I first met you when you were four. She brought you in after your car accident. You'd been so badly broken. You were in the hospital for a long time."

Christopher had to stop and swallow. God. He looked up at her.

"I'm okay now. Played softball in college. Run on a regular basis. Some pain and I have to keep strong, but I'm okay."

He loved how she'd know what he needed to hear. He nodded and continued reading.

"You started therapy in the city, but it was too far to go and finally, she had to bring you in. I'd never questioned why she waited. I figured she felt awkward bringing her child to an ex. But the moment you came in, with your crutches and your casts and that determined look on your face, I fell in love instantly. Probably because you looked just like her—those big blue eyes were always my weakness. And I got to see her again. I made her promise that she would keep bringing you in to see me. I wanted to take care of you from the first second."

Christopher stopped again and looked up. He knew what Patrick meant about those big blue eyes. Damn. Right now they were going to rip his heart out. She looked so sad.

"Regan—"

"Finish it," she said softly. "Please."

He nodded. "Okay." He turned back to the letter. "Then you moved to Bad and I was happier than I'd ever been. It felt so good having you both just a few blocks away and seeing you both around town.

But, finally, your mom had to tell me you were mine. And like I said, it felt right. You had always been like a daughter to me.

Your mother confessed that she'd known I never wanted kids and that all of the reasons she hadn't wanted to be married were still there so she hadn't told me. She thought we were both happier that way. And maybe she was right. God knows I would have been a miserable father—I'm a workaholic, I'm gone from home seventeen hours a day or more, I travel a lot, I'm...fully married to my job. And your mom—as much as I loved her—would have been difficult to live with. I wouldn't have had the time or energy to give her as a husband and as a support system for her condition. That would have just hurt all of us. I think that it all worked out for the best. I got to see you grow up, I got to know you, take care of you, be there for the good times like performances and graduations. But I didn't let you down. I didn't disappoint you or hurt you.

"I know it might not feel like the right decision to you, but it was for your mom and me. I hope you can forgive us for anything you think we did wrong."

The knot in Christopher's stomach tightened and he had to relax his hand so as not to crumple the letter.

This wasn't the Patrick he'd known. The Patrick he'd known, and looked up to, had been fully dedicated to his work, yes. But he was also a loving, generous, kindhearted man besides being a physical therapist. He cared about more than people's physical ailments. How could he say that he thought he wouldn't have been a good husband? That his work was too important? That he couldn't have supported Regan's mother's condition—whatever it was? And how could he not want to be there for more than the good events in Regan's life?

Patrick sounded like...Christopher's father.

His father had been fully committed to his work too. Still was. That meant long hours away from home, taking care of other people while missing things in his own family's life—he'd missed ball games and lost teeth and new puppies. He hadn't even been the one to patch up his own kids. Christopher's brother had broken at least four bones in his life. Christopher had needed stitches twice and had severely sprained his ankle in a basketball game in high school. His father hadn't been there for any of those.

Christopher stared at the letter. He'd looked up to Patrick because he was *different* from his father. Patrick had been called to physical therapy like Christopher had. He had more time with his patients, he got to know them better, he saw them over and over. Patrick had a practice, a career, that Christopher had thought he wanted.

But Patrick also had some not so great things in common with the man Christopher wanted to be *least* like.

"Is that all?"

Regan's soft voice pulled him from his own spinning thoughts. He took a deep breath and shook his head. "Not quite."

He swallowed hard and finished the letter. "I know I don't have a right to ask you for anything, but I'm going to anyway," Christopher continued. "You remember me talking to you about Chri—Christopher Gilmore." He stumbled over his own name and had to swallow again. "I want you to get to know him. I know that sounds crazy, but Christopher is someone I trust completely, someone who has a heart like mine. I would love for you to spend some time with him besides just the clinic, if you both choose to keep it. I took care of you from a distance for a long time, Regan. I'd like to know that someone else is taking care of you now that I'll be gone. You are strong, you are independent, and intelligent, and talented. Somehow. Your mother and I didn't do a good job of making you feel very secure. We didn't do a good job of showering you with the love and attention that you deserve. I want you to have that now. I've never played matchmaker before but since this is my last chance, I'm going to do it for the two people I love most. Give Christopher a chance to give you what you've always needed.

"I love you, Regan. Above all else, I want you to know that.

"Patrick."

CHAPTER SIX

CHRISTOPHER DIDN'T LOOK UP RIGHT AWAY when he'd finished. Reading about himself and Patrick's hope that Christopher could give Regan what she'd always needed and deserved had been strange.

"Hey."

Her soft voice pulled his gaze away from the letter. He looked up.

"You okay?"

She was asking him if he was okay. He gave a short laugh. "Not really."

Regan hugged her arms tighter. "This is awkward."

Awkward wasn't the word he'd use. Reading Patrick saying Christopher had a heart like his and then, in the same letter, learning that Patrick had never wanted to be a father, had never pushed to have more of a relationship with Regan, made Christopher's chest tight and his stomach cramp. He'd looked up to Patrick. He'd wanted to *be* Patrick. And now...

"I'm sorry," Christopher said sincerely. "Maybe I shouldn't have pushed you to read this. I guess this isn't that helpful at all."

She looked puzzled for a moment. "This is very helpful."

"How?"

"It's an explanation."

"But...he didn't want to be a real father. He didn't want to be there. His work was more important than you were."

Regan came forward a few steps. "And if he didn't want to be there and his work was more important, then I'm glad he wasn't around and disappointing me," she said. "I was better off without the constant rejection, don't you think?"

Christopher looked at her, processing that. She might have a point. He definitely knew what it felt like to have his father choose his patients and his work over his family time and time again.

"My dad is a surgeon," Christopher said, for some reason wanting to connect with her on this, to let her know he got it. "He's completely married to his work. Never home. When he is home, he's distracted, on the phone, doing research. He came to watch me play ball maybe two games each season. Each time I knew he was there, I was so nervous, wanting to do so well, that I completely screwed up. The games he came to were my worst ones. Every time. I actually got to the point where I was glad when he didn't show up."

She moved in closer. "When I was little, I pretended my dad was an international spy and that's why he was never around," she said. "I imagined him traveling the world and saving us all from the bad guys. I told myself that he was doing it to keep me safe and keeping everyone else safe in the process. That was a lot easier to take than knowing my dad lived up the street and just didn't want to be around."

Christopher felt a little of the tightness leave his chest as he nodded. "Yeah. It sucks to be last priority."

She was quiet for a long moment. "It's his loss."

"Definitely," he agreed. He shook his head. "I don't get how Patrick could even kind of know you and not want to be around you all the time. I haven't even known you for twenty-four hours and I was even missing you a little when I was just downstairs."

Her eyes grew round.

"What?" Christopher asked. Was that too much? In light of Patrick's self-proclaimed matchmaking, he didn't really think so, but maybe Regan wasn't the leap-of-faith kind of girl.

"I meant *your* dad," she finally said. "It's *his* loss that he's not around more."

Christopher felt his heart thump against his sternum. Looking into her eyes, he slowly nodded. "Yeah, it is. Thanks for saying that."

She came even closer. "Thanks for what you said too."

He sat up straighter and tossed the letter onto the coffee table. "I meant it. This wasn't the guy I knew, or thought I knew. Patrick was...loving. Generous. I can't believe he'd half-ass a relationship with his daughter."

"Maybe half-ass was all he had to give."

Christopher nodded. "Apparently." He knew his disgust was evident in his tone.

"And that's part of what you don't get, right?" she asked, coming to stand right in front of him, between his knees and the coffee table. "You don't understand how to half-ass things, do you?"

"I half-ass cooking dinner most nights."

She gave him a smile that made him want to pull her into his lap.

"Good to know."

"And I half-ass making the bed. I figure I'll just be getting back into it as soon as possible."

And there he saw what he'd been hoping for—a flash of heat in her eyes.

"I'm sorry about the matchmaking thing," she said. "That's what I meant was awkward."

"I'm a little sorry about that too," he said.

A flicker of disappointment crossed her face. "Yeah?"

"He should have done it a long time ago," Christopher said, reaching for one of her hands.

Her arms fell and she let him take her hand and pull her closer, to stand between his knees.

She gave him a smile. "I was away when you were here. Then you were gone by the time I came home."

"Still feels like he waited too long to introduce us."

She took a deep breath and shook her head. "Wow. There's just no way I can help it."

"Help what?"

"This." She climbed into his lap, straddling his thighs, took his face in her hands and kissed him.

She felt so right in his arms, so good against him, that Christopher just took a huge contented breath and then dove into the kiss right along with her.

He opened his mouth, tracing his tongue over her lower lip and then stroking deep when she opened. He held her ass in his hands, squeezing and pressing her more fully against his erection. She sighed in his mouth and Christopher knew he wasn't going to stop until he'd had her again. Right here, right now.

Screw decorum or appropriateness. So they were in Patrick's apartment. So they were here for much more somber activities than sex.

If anything good could come from all of this—his trip back to Bad, Patrick's letters, the whole situation—then it was this. Christopher and Regan could make each other feel all of the things that they both needed to feel. Wanted, appreciated, cared for. They didn't need their fathers or their mentors.

Christopher pulled back to look up into her eyes. "I want you."

"I want you too."

"Here. Now."

She nodded. "Yes."

That was all he needed to hear. He stripped her shirt up and over her head, flinging it away. Her bra followed seconds later.

It was full daylight and Patrick's apartment had nice big windows. Christopher was very grateful to the architect who had put those in and had them facing west, where as much sunlight as possible came in this time of day.

"You are absolutely gorgeous," Christopher told Regan gruffly, taking her breasts in his hands and thumbing over her nipples.

She moaned and arched closer. "Yes, more of that."

He complied for several long, delicious seconds before dipping his head and taking one tip in his mouth. He remembered everything about how she felt, tasted and sounded from the night before. Now he could see it all too. He was already addicted.

"You too now," she said breathlessly.

She tugged at his shirt and Christopher reluctantly let go of her long enough to pull it off.

Regan ran her hands over his shoulders and chest, her gaze following. "God you're hot."

He chuckled. He had never been insecure about his looks but he wasn't sure he'd ever appreciated a compliment as much as that one. "I *am* hot. You're burning me up."

She gave him a cute smile, just before leaning in and rubbing her chest against his. He blew out a breath. There was nothing like the feeling of hard nipples against his chest. He cupped the back of her head and dragged her mouth to his, kissing her hot and deep.

He played with her nipples and kissed her until she was wiggling against him. "Need more of you," he told her roughly.

"Yes. Me too."

"Race you," he told her with a grin.

She matched it as she pushed up off of his lap and stood in front of him, sliding her jeans and panties over her hips, down her thighs and kicking them to the side.

Christopher froze with his jeans open. That was as far as he got before Regan was standing in front of him, completely naked, looking like every hot fantasy he'd ever had.

He remembered everything about how she felt last night in the dark, but having the visual too was like heaven.

"You're…"

"Naked," she filled in. "And you're not."

She bent over and reached for the top of his jeans. He lifted his ass as she tugged them down, hooking her fingers in his underwear at the same time and pulling it all to his knees. He was mesmerized by the sway of her breasts and the curve of her hips and the gorgeous spot between her legs that had his tongue tingling.

But the tongue tingling thing must have been contagious because the next thing he knew, Regan had wrapped her hand around his shaft and was running her tongue over the head of his cock.

His hips bucked and he sucked in a quick breath.

She knelt between his knees and looked up at him as she opened her mouth and then took him deep.

Christopher's breath hissed out and he grasped the back of her head, tangling her hair with his fingers. "Regan—" But he had nothing else.

She moved up and down on him, grasping him low, sliding him in and out with the perfect amount of pressure and suction.

It was one of the hottest things Christopher had experienced. He'd had blow jobs. Good ones. Great ones even—because it was pretty hard for a blow job to not be great. But this one…he had no idea why, but this one was far and away the best.

"Ride me," he said, tugging on her hair. "Want inside you."

She lifted her head, keeping hold of him. "Condom?"

"Pocket. Front. Right." So he'd been hopeful about today.

She grinned and dug for the condom. She pulled it out, ripped it open and rolled it on.

Christopher greedily pulled her back into his lap. "You ready, Cupcake?"

"So ready," she assured him.

"Have to be sure." He lifted her so she was kneeling over him, a knee on either side of his thighs. He ran a hand between her legs, relishing the wet heat.

Her hands were on his shoulders, balancing her, and she gripped him tighter. "Yes. I'm ready, Christopher."

"Patience, sweet thing." He ran his finger over her slick folds then pressed into her.

She tipped her head back with a little sigh.

Christopher watched her face as he stroked in and out, wanting to make her mindless and hungry. He circled his thumb over her clit and felt the resultant tightening around his finger. Her nails dug into his shoulders slightly and he grinned. That was exactly what he wanted.

He leaned in and took a nipple into his mouth, licking then sucking, and she began moving her hips with his finger.

Planning to take her over the edge like this before pulling her down on his aching cock, Christopher was surprised when she pushed his hand away and took his cock in hand, positioning him so she could sink down on him. The friction and heat made him grit his teeth and he gripped her hips, keeping her still for a moment. If she so much as clenched her butt, he was going to be done for.

"Christopher," she said softly, need in her voice.

"I know, sweets, I know," he told her. He breathed in through his nose and out through his mouth three times, working to get some control.

"Need you. Please."

"It won't last long."

"Don't care."

He looked up at her. She bent her head and kissed him.

"It's not like this is the last or only time," she said against his lips. "Take me. Please."

With a groan, he wrapped his arms around her, buried his face in her neck and pumped up into her. Her arms went around his neck and she met his thrust and from there it was all he could do to just hold on for the ride. She took every one of his hard, hot thrusts, her body gripping him, demanding he give her everything, and it was only a few minutes later that he felt her orgasm grab her and felt his own roaring through his body.

After they'd both gone over the top, they sat wrapped around each other, just holding on, breathing hard, their hearts pounding.

A long time later—fifteen minutes or maybe a year—Regan finally lifted her head from his shoulder.

She looked down at him through her tousled hair. Her cheeks were still flushed and she had a sleepy, happy look on her face. "I'm hungry."

Not the words he'd been expecting. He laughed and squeezed her ass. "For food?"

She grinned. "For now."

"What should we do about that?"

She looked a little shy when she said, "You could come to my place. I don't have any roommates. You could…stay…with me… while you're here. You know, save some money on your room."

He put his nose against her collarbone and took a deep breath. "Does the whole place smell like cupcakes?"

She squirmed against him and he was glad to know that even the simple contact had an effect on her too. "I will make you cupcakes every single day you're here if you keep giving me orgasms. Deal?"

He kissed her collarbone then licked along it. "Deal. For sure. No problem. Let's go now."

They managed to separate, deal with the condom, clean up a bit and get redressed without ending up right back on the couch. At the door, Christopher took her hand.

She looked up, surprised, but clearly pleased.

"We've got a lot of work to do," he said.

She nodded. "It'll all still be here tomorrow."

And so would he. Christopher just wasn't sure how many tomorrows there would be.

Patrick had essentially given Christopher half his practice. Christopher could step in and take over and never miss a beat. That was what he'd dreamed of doing at one time. He had a practice in Omaha that was successful, but if someone had asked him even two days ago what his ideal setup would be, it would have been this practice, right here in this town. Beside Patrick, of course. But even without Patrick, Christopher could picture a lifelong practice of caring for friends and neighbors in Bad.

And now Regan was in the picture.

It was far too soon to say that she would be an ongoing part of his life as a business partner or if he'd be making a life *with* her. And yet, it didn't feel crazy to think that might happen.

Not even twenty-four hours after meeting her?

But yes, he couldn't deny it.

What was bugging him was the idea that his mentor hadn't been the man Christopher always imagined. He wasn't a saint, he didn't know everything, he wasn't an altruistic role model for making the right decisions. He'd messed up. He'd made a big mistake. Not by getting Regan's mom pregnant, but in not being a dad to Regan.

Christopher was having a hard time dealing with that.

What else didn't he know about Patrick? Was his vision of Patrick being a great, beloved therapist naïve? Was it just what Christopher had wanted to see because Patrick had seemed so different from his own father? Did he really want to follow in the man's footsteps after all?

He was determined over the next several days to not look at Patrick's office and belongings as those of a man he'd admired, but with the rose-colored glasses removed. He wanted to see what he could find out, see if he could get a sense of who Patrick really was, before he decided what to do with the practice.

"Christopher?" Regan tugged on his hand.

Regan.

Looking down at her now, Christopher knew that, no matter what else he discovered, no matter what illusions were shattered, he would never regret this trip or be upset with Patrick for bringing him back here.

"You with me?" she asked, looking at him as if she knew his thoughts were spinning.

"I'm all yours," he told her. He wasn't coming back to the house and office tomorrow for Patrick. He was coming for some answers because of the woman beside him.

"Then I have some ideas for you," she said.

He started to lean in for a kiss.

"After pizza," she told him, pressing a finger against his lips.

He grabbed her wrist and sucked the tip of her finger into his mouth.

Her pupils dilated and she took a deep breath. "We can get delivery."

Christopher tucked her up against his side and pulled the door to Patrick's apartment shut.

He was definitely all hers now.

They managed to call and place the pizza order before they ended up naked on Regan's bed. The pizza was going to take nearly an hour to get there, so they took their time playing, running their hands and mouths all over each other, teasing and talking, laughing and moaning.

It was glorious.

Regan wasn't sure when she'd last had so much *fun* with sex. In fact, she was having a little trouble clearly remembering the last time she'd had sex at all.

It had been a while.

They'd gotten as far as the shower before the pizza from Bad Brews showed up and Christopher had left her limp against the wall of the shower stall with a huge, smug grin and a towel wrapped around his waist while he went to answer the door.

Regan wasn't sure who had delivered tonight, but it wouldn't surprise her to find out that news had gotten around town that Regan's door had been answered by a half-naked man.

And watching Christopher drop the towel and climb back into the shower with her, she didn't care one bit who knew about him.

He was...unexpected. For sure. But he was wonderful and, in spite of her best efforts to *not* think about it, she couldn't help thinking that him joining her in the practice and staying in Bad wouldn't be all bad. Not bad at all.

But this was all really fast and Christopher hadn't come to town expecting to inherit a half a PT practice. He had his own practice back in Nebraska. And they'd just met. Even if she thought he was having a really good time with her and even if they would probably date if they both lived in the same place, it wasn't like she could expect to be a part of some huge life-changing decision to leave home and move to Bad.

But she wanted to be.

That was the craziest thing of all. She wanted to be at least a small temptation for him.

She hadn't even known him for a full twenty-four hours yet and she already felt a connection to him that would break her heart a little when it was finally time for him to leave.

"So growing up, you never asked your mom about your dad or talked to her about him?"

They were lounging on her bed, covered only with bedsheets, a half-eaten pizza between them, talking.

It was one of the nicest times Regan had ever spent in her bed. And she was a big fan of things that happened in that bed—sex (though again, she couldn't quite recall the last time that had happened), sleep and, of course, Netflix movie marathons.

Naked pizza with Christopher was definitely on top of the list though now.

"My mom...doesn't do well with confrontation or emotional issues," Regan said carefully. Then she sighed. "She's bipolar. She's on medication, goes to therapy, and really, really tries. But she wasn't always as stable as she is now. And even now I treat her with kid gloves. Walk on eggshells. All of that. She would get really upset whenever I would say anything about my dad or if I would ask questions. And I don't even know if all of it is her bipolar disorder. She's very emotional and dramatic even when the medication is working well, so she might have been like that anyway."

Regan ran a fingertip along the edge of her comforter that Christopher said reminded him of the top of a cupcake. It was white and swirled with pink and blue and yellow and green. He'd grinned when he'd first walked into her bedroom and seen it. She loved that grin. It was full of humor and sexy teasing and was far better than the expressions she'd seen at Patrick's apartment. Christopher had been angry on her behalf, which was nice, and surprised and disappointed about the things he'd learned from Patrick's letter to Regan. He'd learned things about his hero today that had taken some shine off of his time in Bad in the past and it made Regan's heart ache.

Another sign that she was getting in really deep really fast with this guy. She could read his expressions and she was feeling a lot of protectiveness and worry on his behalf.

Crazy stuff.

Also crazy was how much she liked talking to him about her mom and childhood. Well, maybe she didn't *like* it exactly but it felt good. He'd told her about his dad—who sounded like a controlling asshole who Regan wouldn't like much—his mother and his older brothers. Now they were on her stuff.

"I remember as a little kid, maybe even before I went to school, just knowing that "dad" was a trigger word. I've wondered since finding out about Patrick if it was because she loved him and missed him, or if she was upset with him, or if she *didn't* love him and having a kid with him was like some horrible mistake she regretted. I don't really know. It just... doesn't matter," she said with a sigh. "It's not worth upsetting her over. He's gone. My life is what it is. I'd rather move forward than look back. I'd rather look at what I have than think about what I don't."

He ran a hand over the arch of her foot. "Now *that* sounds like your dad," he said. "Patrick was the eternal optimist."

She nodded, watching Christopher's face. "He was. Or he seemed like it."

Christopher was looking at her big toe. He frowned at her words but said nothing.

"I know that you found out some stuff today that you didn't like," Regan said. "I'm sure that was hard."

He nodded. "I'm just feeling skeptical about some things, second-guessing some things, that have been these constant guiding ideas for a long time. It's...strange. I thought I knew exactly what I wanted."

"Why does finding out Patrick was an absentee father change any of that?"

He took a breath and looked up. "The first time I met Patrick, he strode into the room, looked me in the eye and said, 'Why do you want to be a PT?'. I said 'because I want to help people'. He scoffed and shook his head and said, 'That's the lazy answer. You can help people in a million ways. You could teach, you could do their taxes, you could fix their plumbing. Physical therapy isn't the only way to help people'. He knew I wasn't being honest and he called me on it. I respected him from that day on."

Christopher was one of the most attractive men she'd ever been with, but there was something about looking into his face while he talked and teased and laughed that tempted her even more than his physical looks. Watching him now, Regan realized there was a feeling of familiarity there. Like she'd known him forever and he had been telling her stories all her life. She loved seeing the different emotions play across his features, loved the details, like the way his mouth curved up on the right a millisecond before the left when he smiled and the way his throat moved when he swallowed. How could *that* be sexy?

"What was the honest answer?" she asked.

He gave a self-deprecating smile and shook his head. "I went to PT school to piss my dad off."

She laughed. "Really?"

"He didn't think I had what it took to be a physician. So I went pre-med. Aced all my classes. Then I found PT and knew *that* would really piss him off. But he didn't get it. He didn't—doesn't—get *me*." He paused. "Patrick did."

Regan's smile died. She felt a definite "aww" feeling come over her and she wanted to hug him.

"No wonder he was important to you," she said.

Christopher nodded, his hand absently rubbing over the top of her foot to her ankle and back. "He was the first person to say he believed that I could do what I wanted to do. And it's strange. I never realized that no one else had ever said that until Patrick did."

Okay, she couldn't *not* hug him. Regan moved the pizza box to the floor then shifted on the bed to lie next to Christopher, stretching out beside him. She put a hand on his shoulder. "He was still that guy, Christopher," she said, looking into his eyes. "You met another side of him today with my letter, I know, but he was still that guy who believed in you and knew you'd be a great PT."

Christopher nodded slowly. "Yeah, I guess so."

"Why are you still looking sad then?" she asked, trying to coax a smile.

He seemed to shake off his melancholy and there was a suddenly twinkle in his eye. "I don't know. Do you have any ideas about how to make me feel better?"

Okay, if that's what he wanted, to ignore all the confusing emotions over Patrick and the situation they were now in, she could do that. They didn't really know each other well enough to spill all their feelings and secrets. And that was assuming they even knew what all they were feeling. She was still reeling from everything too.

"I think I might have some ideas," she said. She wiggled, letting the sheet slide down below her breasts.

"Yep, you do," Christopher told her. "I'm feeling better already."

CHAPTER SEVEN

THE NEXT THREE days were much nicer than Regan ever would have believed. Christopher stayed with her and they had breakfast together before heading over to Patrick's place. They worked on going through things in separate parts of the building, but periodically would bring something to show the other, or one of them would wander to the other's area to take a break.

It was quickly clear that Patrick's professional and personal life had overlapped constantly, in nearly every way. Christopher found multiple photographs, letters and other personal items mixed in with professional things in Patrick's office. Regan found everything from unlabeled x-rays to actual patient files in Patrick's apartment. So rather than dividing things by "personal" and "professional" they simply kept with "upstairs" and "downstairs". Then when they were ready to call it a day, they'd go back to Regan's and make dinner, eat and talk, and then head to bed where they had hot, sweet, amazing sex until they fell asleep together.

It felt like they'd been doing all of it forever and Regan had to constantly remind herself not to get too attached to the routine and the warm fuzzy feelings and, well, Christopher. He was here for a purpose. A purpose that might have an end point. An end point that was getting closer and closer all the time. They hadn't talked about whether he was staying or not.

Until they were eating lunch on the fourth day together and talking about what would happen the following week when Regan's leave from work ended.

"I've had two phone calls about the practice. Two offers to buy," Christopher told her over burgers at the diner.

Regan paused in mid-chew. She swallowed hard. "You have?"

He didn't look happy about it, but he nodded. "They found out Patrick passed and that the ownership is in the air. I don't know how."

"It's a small town," Regan said with a shrug. She was never surprised when people knew things in Bad. It was more unusual for someone to *not* know something.

"One is a PT out of New Orleans who is looking for a second location. The other is a company out of Lake Charles. The clinic would become part of their network of clinics."

Regan tried not to look as crestfallen as she suddenly felt. All along she'd known the possibility of Christopher staying was small. Of course it was. He hadn't come to Bad with this in mind. He'd shared with her that he'd been expecting some meaningful but small memento from Patrick. Not his practice.

She could, of course, keep it and buy Christopher out. Her friend Destiny worked at the clinic part-time and Regan could offer her full-time hours. She could also hire another PT or a couple of PT Assistants.

Still, hearing Christopher talk about giving it up made her sad. And it felt wrong.

She'd only known him for a few days, but they'd been spending twenty-four-seven together for the most part. They'd done a lot of talking and sharing in that time.

And, interestingly, spending that time with Christopher, listening to his stories about PT school and then his time with Patrick, listening to him talk about his past patients, had all made her miss Patrick a little less. And understand him a little more.

She could tell what kind of person, and therapist, Christopher was and she knew personally what kind of therapist Patrick had been. It had been his whole life, that was almost painfully clear, but it had also been his heart. He hadn't dedicated everything he had to his work because of money or power or some sense of ego. He'd done it because he'd loved it. He'd lived it because it *was* him. Being a PT was as much a part of Patrick Faucheaux as his blue eyes—that she now saw every time she looked in a mirror.

She could see what Patrick had seen in Christopher.

Christopher was every good part of Patrick.

"You should stay," she blurted out.

It wasn't until she'd spoken that she realized Christopher had been talking and she hadn't heard a word and she had just rudely cut him off. But she couldn't hold those words in any longer.

"What?" he asked, a french fry suspended in his fingers.

"You should stay here. It's half yours. It has everything you've always wanted and it's...*yours*. The practice has a spirit to it and you...fit. You're the perfect one. These other therapists don't know this town, they didn't know Patrick, they won't know how Patrick and Bad would want that clinic to function. The company will take over and make it corporate and probably rotate therapists through there. And yes, they'll probably all do a fine job. But they won't put their hearts into it and they won't keep Patrick's heart in it."

She stopped and pressed her lips together, realizing that she'd been babbling. About Patrick's practice and his dedication to it—the thing that had kept him from being a father to her in many important ways. Patrick hadn't been able to give his heart to his daughter because he'd already given it to his work.

And now she was telling Christopher he should do the same thing.

But it was true. Christopher belonged here.

Strange as that sounded.

Christopher was looking at her, clearly a bit perplexed. "You're defending him. You're telling me to be like him?"

She sighed. "You *are* like him, Christopher. In all the good ways. He'd be so proud of you. And the only thing that makes sense is you staying here. I know it would mean moving here and leaving Omaha and your family but..." She trailed off.

She wanted him here. But would that matter to him? And if it did, it would mean her taking a risk that Christopher might be like Patrick in *every* way and decide that the practice was more important than being involved in her life. And if *that* happened, it would mean living with that heartache...and seeing him all the time.

And if her wanting him to stay *didn't* matter, she didn't want to hear it.

But Christopher wasn't going to let her off that easy. He put his fry down and reached across the table and snagged her hand. "Regan."

She was studying the glob of ranch on her salad.

"Look at me, Cupcake."

Dammit, she had no choice. She looked up.

"But what?"

He was going to make her finish that. Crap.

"But it's a big decision," she said.

He shook his head. "That wasn't what you were going to say."

He'd known her for four days. How did he know her so well already? "How can you be sure?"

"Because you would have said that. You wouldn't have cut that off."

"Maybe I just lost my train of thought."

He shook his head again. "Come on, Cupcake. Give me the rest. I want to hear it. I *need* to hear it."

Something about that made her heart thump a little

harder. She turned her hand and threaded her fingers between his. "How do you know it was good?" she asked. "What if I was going to say 'but if you do, we'll need to break up'?"

A smile tugged at the corner of his mouth. "No way would you be saying that."

"No?"

"You like the sex too much."

She liked *him* too much. This really was a risk to her heart. "So we'll keep sleeping together if you come to Bad?"

"Damn right."

She smiled at his emphatic response.

"And more," he said.

Her heart thumped again. "Yeah?"

He took a breath. "I've definitely been thinking about it, Regan. If I do keep the practice and move here, part of that will be because of you. We'll be partners. In business and in…life. I know that's fast and crazy and…yeah, maybe it won't work out. But I need you to know that you're part of me wanting to be here, and if that's not cool with you, I need to know now before I make this decision."

She had never been in love before and prior to meeting Christopher, she would have never believed it could happen so fast. But right now, sitting in The Bad Egg, where she'd eaten burgers with numerous dates over the years, just down the street from the two-screen movie theater, where she'd also had many dates over the years, she knew that this thing with Christopher was different.

Fast or not, crazy or not, she was falling for him too.

"I don't want you to leave," she told him.

His fingers tightened on hers and then he gave her a full-wattage smile. "That's what I needed to hear."

They finished their lunch quickly because Christopher had some phone calls to make to Omaha.

Regan headed upstairs as soon as they got back, leaving

Christopher in the office. But not before he kissed her sweetly and said, "We'll celebrate tonight."

She smiled up at him. "With cupcakes."

His eyes darkened and Regan felt the corresponding heat low in her body.

"And buttercream frosting," he told her.

"Of course." She turned toward the steps with a little giggle.

"Hey, Regan?"

She stopped with her foot on the bottom step. She looked back at him. "Yeah?"

"Get extra frosting."

Christopher was so tired of sitting on hold on the phone, but at least while he was on hold, he could keep going through Patrick's paperwork and make a bigger dent in the mountain of stuff on Patrick's desk.

It kept his mind off of why he was on hold.

Holy shit. He was taking over Patrick's practice. And he'd essentially told Regan he was falling for her and moving here in part because of her.

Those were each huge things in and of themselves but put together in a spontaneous decision over a burger it was...crazy.

He took a deep breath and refocused.

It was fine.

For one thing, Regan had brought it up first. She'd been the one to say *you should stay*. It's not like he hadn't thought about it, of course. But he'd convinced himself that the anxiety he'd felt over the company from Lake Charles was simply because he'd known Patrick wouldn't want a huge corporation running his practice. Patrick had valued the close, one-on-one relationships he had with his patients and would have hated the idea of a company making decisions based on their bottom line or rotating providers in and out.

The jealousy Christopher had felt for the guy from New Orleans made less sense. The guy would be a great fit. He was young and enthusiastic, and owned a practice about the size of Patrick's. He had a wife and new baby and was ready to settle down somewhere smaller.

Basically, listening to the guy on the phone the other day, all Christopher had been able to think was *that's what I want.*

Of course, he could have it in Omaha. Probably. That had been his goal when he'd decided to go home and open his clinic. But opening a private clinic in a big city was different than in a place like Bad. He'd worked at one of the hospitals first, networked, saved money and had only opened his clinic's doors fourteen months ago. But it still didn't feel quite...right. Which was strange. It was home. It was where his friends and family were. Where he'd grown up.

And still, Omaha didn't feel like Bad did.

Stepping into an established practice where the PT was beloved and admired in a town where he was an outsider should feel intimidating. Patrick's shoes were big, but for some reason, Christopher had no qualms about taking over and doing things Patrick's way and continuing his legacy.

Maybe that was why things were uncomfortable in Omaha... because that wasn't where he was supposed to be.

He put three papers into the *shred later* file and moved two to the *file* pile.

He gritted his teeth as the hold music switched to an instrumental version of a song he'd hated even when it had been original. It was not improved by the added saxophone.

Then he frowned as he studied the paper in front of him.

It was a letter from the state medical board.

It was a letter stating that Patrick was being investigated because of a complaint from a patient that Patrick had been under the influence while treating her.

The letter was dated two years ago.

Christopher shuffled through the papers underneath the

letter, but like all the papers before it, they were in no particular order and nothing else in the stack seemed to pertain to the letter.

There had to be more to it. There had to be more correspondence that would explain what was going on. Christopher reached for another pile.

The secretary for the company in Lake Charles finally came back on the line. "I'm sorry, Dr. Gilmore, Mr. Waters will be a few more minutes."

"That's okay," Christopher said. "I'll call back." He hung up before she could say anything more.

With both hands now free, Christopher dug through the papers on Patrick's desk, the two stacks next to the desk and one of his three filing cabinets.

Finally, he found what he was looking for.

Two years ago, a patient had reported Patrick for treating her with alcohol on his breath. The patient had called him around six at night saying she was having horrible back pain. Patrick had met her at the clinic. He'd stated to the investigators that he'd had a drink at dinner about ten minutes prior to the patient calling. It was determined through the investigation that Patrick saved the woman's life by recognizing her signs of heart attack and calling the paramedics.

However, there were also testimonies included that indicated Patrick was a regular drinker and that this was not, perhaps, the first time he'd treated a patient while under the influence. He was fined and had to attend chemical-dependency training for six months, with his license on probation during that time.

Christopher was pulled away from the file by a voice from the front of the clinic.

"Hello? Is anyone here?"

Christopher pushed out of the chair, grateful for something to take his mind off of the discovery of Patrick's drinking and poor judgement. He strode down the hallway toward the front desk. "Can I help you?"

"Hi, are you the new physical therapist?" It was a woman, in her mid-twenties, with a little boy of about six.

Was he the new physical therapist? He wanted to be. He was pretty sure. But it seemed every time he'd made a decision, something new came up that made him question it. "I'm *a* PT," Christopher said. "I'm Dr. Gilmore."

"Oh, thank goodness!" the woman said. "I didn't know what was happening with the clinic or anything. I was hoping someone could look at my son's leg. Patrick was seeing him..." She trailed off, looking uncomfortable and like she might cry.

The clinic had been closed for the last few days as Regan dealt with Patrick's affairs and Christopher wasn't sure who was answering any calls that came in.

Christopher immediately knelt in front of the little boy. "What's your name?"

"Noah."

"Hi, Noah, I'm Christopher. What's going on with your leg?"

"It hurts."

"It hurts all the time," his mother said. "He complains about it every day."

"Where on your leg?" Christopher asked.

"My ankle and my knee," Noah said.

"Dr. Faucheaux said he needed more exercise. He thought the problem was because Noah is a little heavy," the woman explained. "But it's not getting better. He's lost a little weight but he still has trouble. And now he doesn't want to go out and play because it hurts so I'm afraid he'll gain it back."

Christopher frowned. "How long's it been going on?"

"Oh two or three months."

Well, shit. Kids didn't have muscular pain that lasted that long and certainly not every day. "Can I look at your ankles, Noah?" Christopher asked.

The boy nodded and Christopher pulled up the bottom of his jeans. "Does his ankle swell like this all the time?"

"Is it swollen?" his mom asked. "I guess I thought it was just because he's a little pudgy."

Christopher swept Noah up and started for an exam room. "Let's take a look."

The kid wasn't pudgy. He was swollen because something was wrong with his joints.

"Hey, Holly."

Christopher heard Regan's voice behind them. He and the woman both turned.

"Hi, Regan."

"What's going on?"

"I know you're closed, but I was hoping you'd be here," Holly said. "It's Noah's leg again."

"Christopher and I were asked to go through Patrick's things," Regan said. "So we're here even though the clinic is officially closed."

"Oh, yeah, I heard..." Holly trailed off, suddenly uncomfortable. "I'm sorry."

Regan gave her a smile. "It's okay, actually. Getting better."

"I'm glad."

"Have you treated Noah?" Christopher asked Regan, cutting in.

"No." She smiled at the little boy. "He's one of Patrick's patients. I just say hi to him when he comes in." Noah grinned at her. "But Christopher is going to be here now," she told Holly. "So I'm glad you're getting to know him. He'll be happy to take over with Noah." Regan met Christopher's eyes and she gave him a smile. "You're in good hands."

"Oh, I'm so glad things are getting settled," Holly said. "Everyone's been wondering what's going to happen."

Regan nodded. "We're going to be fine. Better than fine. Christopher is going to take really good care of us."

Well...hell. That's what he wanted. And of course she would think and say that because the last they'd talked, that had been what Christopher had decided. But now the trepidation was growing again. Dammit.

"Let's check Noah over and see if we can find anything more out," Christopher said, heading into the closest exam room. He set Noah on the exam table and gave the boy a reassuring smile. "I bet Dr. Faucheaux poked around on your legs a lot, didn't he?" he asked.

Noah nodded.

"Would it be okay if I did too?" Christopher needed to start at the beginning. Unless…

"Hey, Regan?" he asked. "Would you be able to pull Noah's chart for me?"

Patrick was still a pen-and-paper kind of guy. Christopher would have to update the system here for electronic medical records but there were times when pen-and-paper charts were kind of nice.

He sighed as he realized that he'd just thought of the new medical records system as a done deal, just like him taking over the clinic seemed a done deal.

"You bet." Regan headed toward the office.

Which was also helpful, since Christopher didn't even know Noah and Holly's last name.

"So it hurts most when he runs and plays?" Christopher asked.

Holly nodded. "Well, and in the morning it seems. He's stiff when he first gets up. Moves slow."

Christopher nodded. "Okay. Noah, I'm going to just check out all your joints move, okay? Do you know what joints are?"

"Where your bones bend," Noah said.

Christopher grinned. "Where two bones meet up and bend. When bones bend they break. We don't want that." It was never too early to teach people how their bodies worked. He pointed to the chart on the wall. "See where those two bones come together?" He pointed to the knee. "That makes the knee joint. Right here." He pointed to Noah's. "And when your knee bends, those bones both move." He bent Noah's knee. It was stiff and swollen. Dammit.

It was clear that Noah had been to the PT a few times—he was very cooperative and didn't fuss with any of Christopher's exam.

Regan came back with his folder. Christopher flipped through it. As he'd suspected, there were no x-rays. Patrick hadn't even referred the kid to a physician.

He explained what he wanted to do to Holly.

"An x-ray? You think there's something wrong with his bones?"

"Actually, no. I think it's the joint. But I want to rule out bone problems too," Christopher explained. "This kind of ongoing pain in a kid Noah's age isn't normal and we need to figure out what's going on. He needs x-rays and blood work."

Holly's eyes got wide. "Blood work?"

Regan stepped closer to her and took her hand. "Holly, relax. Christopher's just being thorough. If something's going on, you want to know, right?"

Holly nodded. "Yes, of course. I just... Dr. Faucheaux never said anything about any of that."

That's what Christopher was most afraid of. Patrick had talked at times about how hard it was to give bad news to people he'd known all their lives and that he would run into at the post office. It was one of the cons of providing healthcare in your small hometown.

Christopher appreciated Regan's presence there. "I want to rule out arthritis and—"

Holly started shaking her head, cutting him off before he got to *bone cancer*.

"Arthritis? He's *six*!"

"Juvenile idiopathic arthritis happens in children under the age of sixteen and—"

"No. No x-ray." She moved to the exam table and lifted Noah into her arms. "I'm sorry, Christopher...Dr. Gilmore. But I don't know you and you're so young and Dr. Faucheaux never said anything about any of this."

"Holly, I understand that what I just said sounds scary but—"

Holly moved toward the door, still shaking her head. "No, I'm sorry. I can't."

Christopher took a breath. He understood where she was coming from but he couldn't let her leave without making sure she understood everything. "Holly, I know you don't know me. But I studied with Dr. Faucheaux and—"

"And you're saying he might be wrong about this and..." She broke off and shook her head again. "No, I'm sorry."

"At least follow up with your doctor," Christopher said. "Let someone take a look at everything. For Noah's sake."

"Holly," Regan said, her voice calm and even. "Just go in and see Brooke and Nick. Just ask them about it. Maybe they'll say Christopher is crazy and overprotective."

Holly pressed her lips together and looked from Christopher to Regan. Then she turned and left the clinic without a word.

They were completely silent for a moment after the door shut behind her. Then Christopher felt the frustration boil up and erupt.

"Son of a bitch!" He slapped Noah's folder on top of the exam table with a loud smack.

"I'll talk to her," Regan said. "She's just worried about Noah. I'll get her to talk to Brooke and Nick."

"Who the fuck are Brooke and Nick?"

"The PA and physician in town." Regan had an eyebrow up though, indicating that he was overreacting.

"If she was worried, she'd be in there getting the x-ray without you having to talk to anyone," Christopher said sharply.

"Christopher, she just met you! She's known Patrick for years!"

He shoved a hand through his hair. Then he blew out a breath. She was right. "I'm sorry. I know that. I'm new, she's worried, I'm telling her that Patrick—" He stopped and gritted his teeth.

"You think Patrick missed something," Regan said.

He nodded. "I do."

Regan took a breath. "Okay, well, JIA isn't common. It's not the first thing you'd think when a six-year-old comes in with a sore knee."

"Ongoing pain over *months*? Six-year-olds get over musculoskeletal pain in hours."

Regan nodded. "Yeah. Okay. But you've made mistakes, haven't you?"

He thought about his answer. Regan had come around over the past few days. She was feeling affectionate towards Patrick, she had gotten her answers—even if they weren't perfect answers, at least she wasn't wondering anymore—and she was feeling more at peace about her relationship with her father. Christopher didn't want to ruin that. His doubts about Patrick were popping up just as Regan was feeling good about him.

"Christopher," Regan said, stepping closer. "Tell me what you're thinking."

"You sure?"

She must have read something in his eyes because she didn't answer right away. Finally she swallowed and nodded. "Yeah, tell me."

"Yes, I've made mistakes. But…"

She frowned. "Christopher, what is it?"

"Patrick was drinking. While he was seeing patients."

"*What*?"

"He was disciplined by the PT board."

"When?"

"Two years ago."

She looked at him as if she hadn't understood anything he'd said.

"You okay?" he asked.

"Are you sure about that?"

He shrugged. "I saw the files on the complaint and the hearing and the discipline."

"But that doesn't mean...he didn't keep doing that."

Christopher hated it as much as she seemed to. He sighed. "I don't know. I hope not."

"Hey, two years ago...weren't you here with him then?"

And *that* got right to something that had been bugging Christopher badly. "Yeah."

"And you didn't know he'd been disciplined?"

"I had no idea."

Regan tipped her head. "Did you ever notice him drinking? Did you ever smell anything on his breath?"

"I saw him have a drink once in a while after hours. Scotch at dinner or something."

"Okay, well, that's not the same thing as drinking on the job."

He knew that. He'd been telling himself the same thing. But the niggling doubt remained. As much as he hated it. "When you're a small-town provider, there is no after-hours," he said. "You never know when people are going to need you. Or, if they do, you have to say no if you're impaired. He didn't."

Regan nodded. "I guess that's true. But...one drink doesn't mean he's impaired. Or that he couldn't do the job. Right?"

"No. It doesn't mean that." He huffed out a breath. "I don't know what it means."

"Isn't it better to assume the best?" she asked. "I mean, he's gone and I..."

Christopher cocked an eyebrow. "What?"

"I want you to remember him the way you did when you first came to town," she said with a sigh.

In spite of his mixed-up emotions, he smiled too. "Yeah?"

"You drove me crazy when we first met at the lawyer's office and you thought Patrick was this huge hero, this perfect guy, and with everything I had found out about him, that was the last thing I wanted to hear. But now... I feel like over the past few days I've gotten to know Patrick better, and even though I think he screwed up not letting me know who he was sooner and being more involved with me, there was still *a lot* of good there. And you were the reason I gave him a chance. And I just really wish you could still feel the way about him that you did when you first came to Bad." She grimaced slightly. "I'm afraid I'm part of why you're feeling less...generous about him."

"You're—" But he couldn't say that she wasn't. He supposed she'd made him look at Patrick more realistically. Patrick falling down as a father had opened Christopher's eyes to the possibility that he wasn't perfect in other ways as well. "My favorite part of this trip," he finished. It was the truth. In spite of his image of Patrick being tarnished, Christopher wouldn't have changed meeting Regan.

But...and he hated that there was a but...the trip had made him think differently about a lot of things. He wondered what other things he had been looking at naively.

Like falling in love.

He hated the thought even as it went through his mind. But he had to admit...falling in love with someone in one day seemed silly and overly optimistic.

Regan stepped closer. "Chri—"

And Christopher took a step back.

CHAPTER EIGHT

REGAN HATED the way her heart seemed to fall to her stomach. "Christopher?"

"I'm sorry. I just...need a second." Christopher shoved his hand through his hair.

"A second for what?"

"To figure out how I'm feeling. And what I want to do."

"What you want to do?" she repeated. "About what?"

"About all of this. Patrick and the clinic and..."

Regan's stomach twisted. "And what?"

"You. Us."

Yeah, that's what she was afraid he was going to say.

"Why are you suddenly so upset?"

"Why are *you* not upset?" he threw back to her. "You just found out that Patrick was drinking and he might have missed a big diagnosis and..." He trailed off, almost as if he'd run out of words.

Regan got it. "*You* just found out another reason to be disappointed in him," she said.

"Yes!" Christopher exclaimed. "Yes, definitely. And why aren't *you* disappointed?"

She shrugged. "Because I didn't have huge expectations of

him prior to all of this. I liked him, I cared about him, I felt close to him, but the pedestal I had him on was much shorter than the one you had him on."

Christopher took a breath and nodded. "Yes, you're exactly right. I did have huge expectations. And for *years* I've been thinking of him as this person I wanted to emulate. Not just as a physician, but as a person. I thought he was the perfect role model in every way. And then I come here, to honor him and his life now that he's gone. And instead I found out that he's not who I thought he was—as a physical therapist or as a man—and I'm now questioning everything. He used to be the one that made sense out of things for me, and now, I'm more confused than I've ever been. Because of him."

Regan had to swallow hard. "You're questioning *everything*?"

She could see the sadness in his eyes, but he still nodded.

Okay. Well, that hurt. But she could understand.

"It's all happened really fast," Christopher said. "And every time I think I've made a decision and I know what to do, I find something else out that makes me wonder." He took a deep breath. "I think I need to take more time. Make sure I really know what I'm getting into."

"With the clinic?" she asked softly.

"With everything."

"Because you think that maybe there are things about me or about being with me that might show up with more time that will make you hesitate." She suddenly felt cold all over. She crossed her arms.

Christopher didn't look happy either. "It's been really fast. It's a huge decision, like you said. Before I pack up and move across the country, I just need to be sure."

"Okay, we'll figure it out."

"I need to go home."

They spoke at the same time.

"Home?" Regan asked after a moment.

"Omaha."

Okay, that *really* hurt.

Damn, talk about a one-eighty.

They were both dealing with a lot. She got that. And she really understood the being disappointed thing. And she knew moving here from Nebraska was a big deal. And…yeah she got it.

But she hated it.

"What are you going to do with the clinic then?" she asked.

"I haven't gotten ahold of the guy in New Orleans yet."

"So you haven't told him that you had decided to keep it yourself."

"No."

Which meant he could still buy Christopher's half and become her partner.

"I don't want another partner. I'll buy you out. I'll call Mr. Benson tomorrow."

"I'm not going to make any big decisions right now. I'm just going to go home for a while. Think about things."

She nodded. Well, that was better than going home and not thinking about things.

"I'll…call you." He started for the door.

Regan shook her head. "Wait, *now*? You're leaving now?"

He didn't turn back but he stopped with his hand on the doorknob. "I have to go now. I can't stay."

Did that mean he thought that if he stayed he wouldn't want to leave?

"Christopher, I—" But she didn't know what to say. That she was in love with him and couldn't imagine being here without him now?

That was crazy. He was right. They should both be second-guessing things.

Third-guessing even.

And if he wanted to go back to Omaha, to bail, to run home, then fine. His loss. But she wanted to kiss him. Hug him. Beg him to stay.

He did glance back after he'd pulled the door open. "You really were the best part of all of this. No matter what else came of this trip, I wouldn't change a minute with you."

Tears threatened. "Don't," she said.

"Don't what?"

"Don't be nice and then walk out. Be an ass and walk out. Or be nice...and stay."

He paused. Then he gave her a single nod. "Your dad was kind of a jerk."

Then he turned and walked out.

Just like she'd asked.

Except that saying Patrick was kind of a jerk wasn't really that ass-ish. Because it was kind of true.

"So you're the guy who's down here getting shit-faced. Thought you were out of town."

Christopher lifted his head and focused on the guy standing in front of his corner table at the Trudy's Tavern, the bar across from St. Anthony's hospital in Omaha. The hospital where he'd started his career.

He loved this bar. It was always full of healthcare workers. People who did what they did for a living because they cared about people and were willing to work their asses off to make those people better.

Like the guy who had just kicked out one of the chairs at Christopher's table and sat without an invitation.

Invitations were kind of an optional thing in Trudy's.

"I'm not in a socializing mood, Sam."

Not that Sam Bradford would care about that.

Trudy owned the place and did most of the bartending. She also knew everyone. Which meant that Trudy was able to tattle on people who were trying to get shit-faced in peace.

Christopher picked up his shot glass and tipped it back. He

hadn't been trying for very long and now that Trudy had called in reinforcements, it looked like his shit-faced-ness was going to be cut short.

Sam was a paramedic at St. A's but everyone at the hospital, especially those who frequented Trudy's, knew Sam and his crew. He'd also been seeing Christopher for a sore shoulder for the past few weeks, which was how he knew about Christopher's trip to Louisiana. He could have stuck with the therapists at the hospital, so it meant a lot to Christopher that Sam had come to his clinic.

Of course, it was a guaranteed, paid-for hour that Sam could give Christopher a hard time so there was that.

"How was the reading of the will?" Sam asked.

"Life changing."

Sam lifted a brow. "How fucking drunk are you?"

"Not enough."

He grabbed one of the three remaining shot glasses in front of Christopher and tipped it back, then cringed. "What the hell is that?"

"A two-fifty-two." Christopher grabbed one before Sam could empty both of the remaining glasses.

"What's that?"

"Bacardi one-fifty-one and Wild Turkey one-o-one."

Sam shuddered. But reached for the last shot glass.

He drank it, shuddered again, and said, "The trip to Bad was that bad?" He smirked at the stupid and unintentional joke.

Christopher stared at his beer bottle. If he'd come to try to forget about Regan and Bad, clearly this wasn't going to do it. "The trip was awesome. And terrible."

"Ah," Sam said. "There was a woman."

Christopher frowned at him. "I didn't say that."

"You didn't have to. Awesome and terrible at the same time, along with life changing—has to be a woman."

Sam was happily married to Dani, who was most definitely awesome. And had certainly changed Sam's life. Stories about

Sam and his crew of paramedics—and best friends—were still told.

"You married guys think you're so smart."

"Ha," Sam said, stretching his legs out underneath the table. "We definitely don't. We've got wives at home reminding us that is *not* true."

Christopher rolled his eyes, but he didn't argue. He had to admit that Dani seemed pretty happy but she definitely didn't let Sam get away with anything.

"So what happened?" Sam asked.

"Trudy called you to counsel me?"

"No, she called me to take you home. But you don't look ready to go yet."

He wasn't. Because he still had enough brain cells to think about and miss Regan.

"Her name is Regan."

"Regan. Pretty."

"Beautiful." Christopher shifted on his chair. "She's Patrick's daughter."

Sam lifted an eyebrow. "Patrick's the PT friend?"

Christopher nodded.

"Interesting."

"Yeah." That was one word.

"You in love with her?"

Christopher snorted. "So fucking in love."

"But you're *here*."

"Yeah."

"The shots make more sense now," Sam decided.

"So you're the guys down here getting shit-faced."

Christopher looked up to find Dooley Miller, another of Sam's crew, taking a chair at the table.

"I thought you were out of town," Dooley said to Christopher as he picked up a shot glass, sniffed it, grimaced, and set it back down.

"Trudy called you too?" Christopher asked.

"Apparently she'd called someone before me, but that someone sat down and started drinking rather than take you home."

"And here you are sitting too," Sam said to Dooley.

"The drinking part was the real concern."

"I only had two shots," Sam said.

So had Christopher. Not nearly enough.

"Uh-huh," Dooley said.

"We were talking about the woman Christopher fell in love with while he was in Bad," Sam said.

Dooley turned an interested look on Christopher. Christopher who didn't have any more shots in front of him. He groaned.

"In love with a Bad girl."

"That joke's too easy," Sam informed him.

"Joke? Come on. Tell me they don't refer to the girls there as Bad girls," Dooley said. "If they don't, they're missing a huge opportunity. They should have t-shirts and shit."

Christopher sighed. "They do."

Dooley grinned. "No shit?"

"They've got a convenience store called Bad Gas. The church is Bad Faith Community Church. The medical clinic is Bad Medicine. And the PT clinic is The Bad Place."

Dooley shook his head, looking almost in awe. "I fucking love this place. I'm going to need *all* the t-shirts. When can we come visit?"

"You're on your own. I'm not going back," Christopher said, aware that he sounded like a pouting five-year-old.

Dooley looked at Sam. "But he's in love."

"I know. But...you know how it is at first."

Dooley nodded. "Oh. It's at first."

"What's that supposed to mean?" Christopher asked, grumpily.

"You're still fighting it, unaware that you're totally fucked and will never win that battle," Dooley said.

"No." Christopher shook his head. "It's not like that. I only knew her for a few days."

There was a moment of silence and then Sam and Dooley both burst into laughter.

Christopher frowned at them. He waited for them to quiet down and then said, "I know what you're going to say."

"Do you?" Dooley asked.

"You're both going to say that you fell in love with your girls within days of meeting them. But that's not normal. *You're* not normal."

They both laughed again.

"I mean, *that's* fair," Dooley said.

"Totally," Sam agreed.

But they didn't deny they'd fallen in love quickly.

And, fucking hell, Christopher couldn't deny that they were not only very much in love years later, but their wives were amazing women who seemed equally in love. And normal, actually.

Christopher had seen it happen over and over—and work out—with a bunch of guys at the hospital. These weren't flings, these weren't lust mistaken for love. These were the real deal.

"So what are you going to do now? You can't do *this* every night," Dooley said.

"Why not?" Christopher took a swig of beer. "I'm going to take my half mil pay-out from Bad and retire."

Dooley whistled. "Haf a mil, huh? Okay then."

"Well, Amanda will be happy to hear that," Sam said.

"Amanda?"

"Amanda? Ryan Kaye's fiance? The PT?" Sam asked.

"Yeah, I know her." Amanda had taught some of the classes he'd taken in PT school as a matter of fact.

"Well she's meeting with someone about joining the practice down in Bad."

Christopher frowned. That made no sense. Or did it? He was a little drunk. "What the hell are you talking about?"

"Some woman came into the hospital looking for the PT department and we steered her toward Amanda's office."

Amanda was the Director of Rehab at St. A's now.

"They got to talking and this woman got Amanda all excited. She said she and Ryan would love Louisiana."

That definitely made no sense. Amanda's entire family was in Omaha and she was incredibly close to them. Ryan was like a brother to his friends and they both loved the city and their jobs. No way would they move to Louisiana.

That's what you thought when you first signed up for that internship.

It was true. He'd signed up to spend one of his rural rotations for school in small town Louisiana to have a completely new experience. He'd figured he could do anything for twelve weeks. He'd thought it'd be fun to see a new part of the country and experience a bit of a new culture.

He hadn't expected to fall in love in Bad.

Twice.

Christopher felt his stomach drop. "Where are they meeting?"

"Right here." Sam pointed.

Christopher swung to look at the bar. Where he saw Amanda Dixon sitting at the bar. Alone.

"She's not with anyone."

"It's someone from out of town," Sam said with a shrug. "Must have gone to the bathroom."

"Seriously?" Christopher got up and stalked to where Amanda was sitting on a barstool, legs crossed, chatting with Trudy. "What the hell is going on?" he demanded.

Amanda turned with both brows up. "Excuse me?"

"You're talking to someone about the clinic in Bad?"

Was she partnering with one of the companies that wanted to buy out the clinic? That might make *some* sense. Maybe Amanda was looking to become an investor. She definitely knew enough about the business to make an excellent manager of a company like that.

But did that mean Regan had decided to sell? The whole thing? Was she giving it up? Was she leaving Bad?

Panic gripped him.

No. Regan needed to be in Bad. She needed to keep the clinic. She needed to take care of her town. She needed to keep The Bad Place in the building with the crazy mural and the ornate ceiling and the gaudy plaster pillars.

More, she needed a chance to have a family legacy and to practice knowing that Patrick had been her father and that the things that made her who she was—her sweetness and her heart, and her passion for helping people, and her patience and empathy, came in part from him. He *had* helped raise her. He had influenced her. He'd mentored her. Even if it hadn't been formal. Even without knowing she was his blood. He'd loved her. He'd been there as much as he could be.

"Yeah. It's a sweet deal. Small practice in desperate need. All set up and ready to go. I've been thinking about getting back into more patient care. I can just walk in and start. The PT before me was beloved. Recently passed away."

A sharp stab of pain pierced Christopher's heart. Sounded far too familiar.

"How'd you find this clinic?"

"She came to me. Said they had something else set up, but it fell through." Amanda took a drink. Her eyes narrowed as she studied Christopher. "You look like hell."

"That makes sense." Then something she said sunk in. "Who was *she* that came to you?"

"Regan Reynolds. She's the PT there now. She's looking for a new partner."

Suddenly there was more coursing through Christopher than liquor and sadness. Now he was pissed. "Regan? You talked to *Regan*?"

"Yep."

"*Regan* is the one talking to you about coming on board?"

"Yes." Amanda said it firmly as if she was talking to a three-year-old. Or a very drunk man.

"Fuck that. That's my practice and *I'm* her partner."

Amanda, used to being around hot-headed men—her brother, her fiancé, and all their friends at the top of that list—barely blinked at Christopher's sudden impassioned statement. "It's yours? I thought you'd changed your mind."

He had. Until the reality of someone else having that clinic was right in front of him. And the idea of someone else being Regan's partner through everything to come was a possibility.

They were his. No question in his mind. Or heart.

"Well, I'm telling you right now, Bad is *mine*."

"Damn right it is."

Christopher spun to find the voice that was so achingly familiar he almost stopped breathing. Regan was here. She was *here*. Right now.

Unfortunately, the liquor combined with the fast spinning was a bad idea. Amanda caught him as he tripped over his own feet.

"Pathetic," Amanda said. "Really."

"Water. Coffee." Trudy pushed a glass and a cup across the bar.

"Ibuprofen?" Amanda asked, handing the water to Christopher.

"You sure you don't want him to hurt *a little* in the morning?" Trudy asked. "Good deterrent."

Christopher barely heard them. He was staring at Regan.

"So this is Regan?" Sam asked, a huge grin stretching over his face.

Christopher nodded. His entire body itched with the urge to touch her, but he held back. Because once he did, he wasn't going to want to stop.

"What are your intentions with our boy here, Regan?" Dooley asked.

Which was hilarious, considering Dooley had had plenty of bad intentions in his past.

"My intention is to confess my love, convince Christopher that he's fine and that his mentor was actually a great guy, and then ask him if we're going to settle down together in Bad or Omaha," Regan said. She glanced at Amanda. "That was kind of mean of you."

Amanda laughed and waved her hand. "Trust me, I know all about stubborn men. Sometimes you have to smack them in the face with the truth. The truth is other people did—*do*—want that clinic. I just made it real and right in front of him instead of people in emails and voicemails."

Regan looked at Christopher. "I got to Omaha and realized I didn't know where you live or where your clinic is. I'd heard you talk about St. Anthony's. So I figured they would know where to find you. I went to the rehab department and met Amanda. She made me spill my guts."

"I love a good love story," Amanda said with a smile.

"Is this a good love story?" Christopher asked no one in particular.

"It sure could be," Regan said. "But a *good* love story, really depends on the ending."

Dooley looked from Christopher to Regan. "You'd really settle down here in Omaha?"

"Do I need to know how to drive a tractor or anything?" she asked.

Sam snorted. "Well, not right away. We'll give you a couple of weeks to learn."

"So, tractor driving lessons take longer than falling in love around here," Regan said.

"Everything takes longer than falling in love around here," Sam said. He gave her a wink and threw an arm around Dooley. "I think we all have somewhere else to be."

"We're going to miss the good part," Dooley said as Sam pulled him toward the door.

"Yeah, well, this is Christopher's good part," Sam said. "Our good parts are at home."

Dooley glanced back at Christopher. "Dude, if Regan is about to give you what I have at home, don't screw it up."

Yeah, Christopher liked that idea.

"And with that," Amanda said, sliding off her stool. "I'm also going to head home to my good part. But—" she said, pausing and pointing a finger at Christopher. "You know better than this. You're a PT for God's sake. And a damned good one. You know very well that things don't have to be perfect to be amazing. In fact, the things that are flawed, and weak, and rough around the edges, are the things that we get up for in the morning and the things that we remember for years to come."

Christopher felt his heart thump hard at that. She was absolutely right. "Thanks, Amanda."

Amanda gave him a smile, then winked at Regan, then left them alone.

Regan climbed up on the stool next to him as the door shut behind his friends.

"Hi," she said simply.

"How long have you been here?"

"At the bar or in town?"

"Either. Both," he said, still trying to convince himself that she was real.

"Got to town about four hours ago. Went to the hospital. Met Amanda. We talked for a while. She conspired with Sam and Dooley. Then brought me here for a drink and convinced me to let you talk things out with Sam and Dooley before telling you I was here."

God, he *ached* for her. How could he miss someone he'd just met so much?

"You were trying to talk Amanda into taking the practice?"

She rolled her eyes. "I was telling her about the practice. She said she knew the perfect way to find out how you really felt about it."

Christopher grabbed the coffee cup and gulped the strong black brew down in three swallows. He was really wishing now that he hadn't taken those shots.

Regan took his hand after he set the coffee cup down. "Christopher, I know that Patrick disappointed you. I know you feel disillusioned. I understand why you might not want to take over the practice now. But before you decide for sure, you have to know that Patrick wasn't perfect, but he *was* a great man and a great physical therapist. And I'm actually *glad* that you learned everything about him."

"Why would you be glad about that?"

"Because it gives *you* permission to not be perfect," she said. "You looked up to him, and all the things you loved about him were true. He was a dedicated, passionate therapist who spent his life taking care of people because he loved it. Nothing you've learned about him changes that. But he was human. You had him up on a huge pedestal and I think, over time, that would have been hard. As you practiced and as you made mistakes sometimes, you would have been comparing yourself to Patrick, and feeling like you were falling short. Now you know the *truth*...that we all mess up, we all make the wrong choices sometimes, but love is what matters in the end. If you do what you do out of love, then you're right...at least in the ways that really count."

Christopher blinked at her. She was right. That was all true.

And even if it wasn't, he would have been going back to Bad with her.

"By the way, Holly took Noah to see Nick at the medical clinic. He suggested x-rays as well," Regan said.

Christopher felt his eyes widen. "So I was right."

Regan shook her head. "No. You were right that an x-ray was a good idea. And there was definitely some swelling. But his blood work came back normal. It's not JIA or cancer. Looks like a stress fracture."

He huffed out a breath. "You know, sometimes I don't mind being wrong."

She smiled and leaned in, putting her hand on the back of his neck. "Holly wants you to do any therapy with Noah once he's healed up. If you come back to Bad."

Oh, he was going back to Bad. He had never felt so good, so *right* about something.

"I love you," he blurted.

The liquor might have loosened his tongue, but he meant those three words with everything in him.

Her face brightened. "I love you too."

"That's crazy," he said.

"Yep."

He chuckled at that simple answer.

"You know," she said. "No matter what else Patrick did or didn't do, messed up or got right, he did do one very good thing."

"Made you?"

She smiled. "Made *us*."

Christopher pulled her in close. "Yeah. He really was a good guy."

She sighed. "He really was a very good Bad guy."

They laughed and Christopher pulled her off her stool as he stood and wrapped his arms around her. He buried his face in her hair and breathed deep.

Buttercream.

"I'm so in the mood for cupcakes," he said gruffly against her ear.

"I thought I saw a bakery on my way to the hospital," Regan teased, pressing close.

"Yes, yes you did."

"You want to swing by there on our way home?" she asked, her eyes twinkling with memories of just how delicious the frosting had been the last time they'd gotten cupcakes.

He looked down at her. "No. But we can swing by there on

our way to my apartment where we're staying tonight. Before we head *home* to Bad."

Her smile was dazzling and she rose on her tiptoes to press a kiss against his lips.

When she pulled back, she asked, "You really feel like you can leave Omaha?"

He nodded. "My clinic and my girlfriend are in Louisiana."

Her eyes got a little shiny at that.

"But..." he said slowly, turning her and starting to walk her backward.

Her brows lifted. "Yes?"

"It just so happens that this bar has a storeroom right around the corner."

Her eyes went wide and a mischievous grin curled her lips. "I have a thing for bad boys though. And you're a really good guy," she said, paraphrasing what he'd said to her the first night at Bad Brews.

He turned her down the short hallway, then reached for the knob on the storeroom door and backed her into the room. As he shut them inside, he said, "Not anymore. I'm very officially a Bad boy now."

Thank you so much for reading Regan and Christopher's story! There's a lot more sexy, fun from Bad!

These books are all standalones and don't need to be read in any particular order!

The Best Bad Boy: (Jase and Priscilla)
A bad boy-good girl, small town romance

Bad Medicine: (Brooke and Nick)
A hot boss, medical, small town romance

Bad Influence: (Marc and Sabrina)
An enemies to lovers, road trip / stuck together, small town romance

Bad Taste in Men: (Luke and Bailey)
A friends to lovers, gettin'-her-groove back, small town romance

Not Such a Bad Guy: (Regan and Christopher)
A one-night-stand, mistaken identity, small town romance

Return of the Bad Boy: (Jackson and Annabelle)
A bad boy-good girl, fake relationship, small town romance

Bad Behavior: (Carter and Lacey)
A bad boy-good girl, second chance small town romance

Got It Bad: (Nolan and Randi)
A nerd-tomboy, opposites attract, small town romance

Find all of my books at
ErinNicholas.com

And join in on all the FAN FUN!

Join my **email list!**
bit.ly/Keep-In-Touch-Erin
(be sure you get those dashes and capital letters in there!)

And be the first to hear about my news, sales, freebies, behind-the-scenes, and more!

Or for even more fun, join my **Super Fan page** on Facebook and chat with me and other super fans every day! Just search Facebook for Erin Nicholas Super Fans!

WANT MORE FROM THE BAYOU?

There's so much more from Erin's Louisiana bayou world!

Head down the road to Autre next and dive into the Boys of the Bayou series (where you'll first meet the Landry family)!

All available now!

My Best Friend's Mardi Gras Wedding

Sweet Home Louisiana

Beauty and the Bayou

Crazy Rich Cajuns

Must Love Alligators

Four Weddings and a Swamp Boat Tour

And be sure to check out **the connected rom com series,**

Boys of the Bayou-Gone Wild

Otterly Irresistible

Heavy Petting

Flipping Love You

Sealed With A Kiss

Say It Like You Mane It

Head Over Hooves

Kiss My Giraffe

And the **Badges of the Bayou** (where you get to know Michael LeClaire and JD Evans!)

Gotta Be Bayou

Bayou With Benefits

Rocked Bayou

Stand Bayou

Stuck Bayou

Just Wanna Be Bayou

And MUCH more—

including my printable booklist— at

ErinNicholas.com

ABOUT ERIN

Erin Nicholas is the New York Times and USA Today bestselling author of over forty sexy contemporary romances. Her stories have been described as toe-curling, enchanting, steamy and fun. She loves to write about reluctant heroes, imperfect heroines and happily ever afters. She lives in the Midwest with her husband who only wants to read the sex scenes in her books, her kids who will never read the sex scenes in her books, and family and friends who say they're shocked by the sex scenes in her books (yeah, right!).

Find her and all her books at
www.ErinNicholas.com

And find her on Facebook, Goodreads, BookBub, and Instagram!

Ingram Content Group UK Ltd.
Milton Keynes UK
UKHW010025300523
422528UK00004B/378